Experimental Phenomenology

Experimental Phenomenology

Multistabilities

Second Edition

DON IHDE

Self-portrait / green by Don Ihde.

Published by State University of New York Press, Albany

© 2012 State University of New York

For information, contact State University of New York Press, Albany, NY
www.sunypress.edu

Production by Ryan Morris
Marketing by Michael Campochiaro

Library of Congress Cataloging-in-Publication Data

Ihde, Don, 1934–
    Experimental phenomenology : multistabilities / Don Ihde. —2nd ed.
        p. cm.
    Includes bibliographical references (p.) and indexes.
    ISBN 978-1-4384-4286-0 (pbk. : alk. paper)
    ISBN 978-1-4384-4285-3 (hardcover : alk. paper)
    1. Phenomenology. I. Title.

B829.5.I33 2012
142'.7—dc23   2011038328

10 9 8 7 6 5 4 3 2 1

For all my international advisees and their dissertations
From which I have learned much.

Contents

List of Illustrations

Preface to the Second Edition

It was over a publisher's lunch, doing drawings of Necker cubes on napkins, enticing for the hosting editor, five perceptual variations on the various cubes, that *Experimental Phenomenology* got its launch into an already long publishing history. It was first with G. P. Putnam's (1977), later SUNY Press (1986) and now it becomes this enlarged second edition, again SUNY Press, 2012. With a more than three decade run, the new edition can be fitted into a somewhat broader context.

The mid-'70s were my own mid-career, when three formative books saw print: *Listening and Voice: A Phenomenology of Sound* (Ohio, 1976), *Experimental Phenomenology: An Introduction* (Putnam's, 1977), and *Technics and Praxis: A Philosophy of Technology* (Reidel, 1979). Each reflected quite self-conscious decisions about what I wanted to do philosophically. In retrospect, I see that I have always been somewhat "contrarian." In the case of *Listening and Voice*, one of my aims was to do a phenomenology, contrary to talking about past phenomenologists or others doing or talking about phenomenology. And, also in some respects, in contrast to the dominant philosophical interests in the visual, I chose auditory experience as the base for practicing phenomenology. Then, very shortly after, I did return to visual experience, but again with a twist by looking at ambiguous visual drawings. Here the contrarian direction was to show how much empirical visual psychology was reductionist with a high emphasis upon bi-stability, at most tri-stability, as in the standard interpretations of perceiving Necker cubes and other illusions. I had worked out a series of perceptual variations that yielded a much larger number of perspectival results and which showed how a phenomenological deconstruction leads to much greater multistability. But I did not then recognize that this search would lead to my own radical antiessentialism, which would later lead to an equally radical transformation of phenomenology itself. Then came *Technics and Praxis*, frequently cited as the first American philosophy of technology book. In that book, I developed an interrelational ontology of human-technology relations, clearly patterned upon phenomenology. This was to be my "material" turn, which to the present remains another signature issue for me. In effect, I had taken "intentionality" to include an extended materiality within our relations with the world. (With this second edition of *Experimental Phenomenology*, two of these three books are now available through our own SUNY system Press.) Indeed, the move to Stony Brook University in 1969, a genuine research university, marked the beginning of a now long books list.

A second retrospective glance back at the first edition can help show what and why the additional material enriches the second edition with its new emphasis upon material multistability: While publishers like to have authors identify who their likely readers will be, I have found this to be a virtually impossible task since my audiences have usually surprised me. Yes, the first edition was primarily designed to *introduce*, better, show *how to do* phenomenology as a *praxis*. The mid-'70s were the times when "continental" philosophies not only were a minoritarian strand within North American philosophy, but often were deliberately dismissed by the dominant strands of "analytic" or Anglo-American philosophy. Yet, it was also clear that there was strong and rising interest among students precisely interested in continental approaches to philosophy, so here a fulfilled designed intent was part of the early positive reception to the first edition. Initial responses from reviewers and others communicating about *Experimental Phenomenology* was that it was clear, filled with concrete and understandable examples, and that it demonstrated a style of phenomenological rigor that was quite philosophically respectable. So far, so good.

The readers I did *not* expect, turned out to come from a wide variety of disciplines which I will here cite by way of particular individuals who in different ways used or "applied" the techniques of experimental phenomenology to various fields. Ference Marton, located in the pedagogical university in Goteborg, Sweden, and himself the founder of *phenomenographical* work, found the experimental ways of introducing phenomenology to be useful for teaching creative thinking and developed a version of experimental phenomenology as a curriculum for secondary students in Swedish high schools—an education application. (*Experimental Phenomenology* has been published in a Swedish translation by Daidalos Press, 2001.)

Another strand related to the natural sciences, including mathematics and physics. I worked with John Marburger III, for a long time Stony Brook's president and himself a physicist, as part of a team for the WISE (Women in Science and Engineering) NSF program. When I used experimental phenomenology examples in our joint classes, he told me he realized that this was a perceptual topology that worked amazingly like topology in mathematics.

Much later, Albert Borgmann, in his contribution to Evan Selinger's *Postphe-nomenology: A Critical Companion to Ihde* (SUNY, 2006), noted the relevance of multistability for both relativity and quantum physics; and, finally, Robert Rosenberger of the Georgia Institute of Technology has noted how multistable readings of science imaging lay at the base of a number of science controversies. His examples related to neurology and the imaging of neurotransmitters, in "A Case Study in the Applied Philosophy of Imaging: The Synaptic Vesicle Debate," *Science, Technology & Human Values* 36(1) (2011), with a second example of distance imaging, "Perceiving Other Planets: Bodily Experience, Interpretation and the Mars Orbiter Camera," *Human Studies* 31(1) (2008). In both cases nonabstract images presented multistable possibilities for theorizing.

Then, in cultural anthropology there are a number of thinkers who began to combine themes from *Experimental Phenomenology* and *Listening and Voice*, for example, Steven M. Friedson in *Dancing Prophets: Musical Experience in Tumbuka Healing* (Chicago, 1996) and Steven Feldman and Keith Basso in *Senses of Place* (School of American Research Advanced Seminar Series, 1996). But the widest and broadest use goes to a variety of interdisciplinary media studies over the years and the globe. Here, Vivian Sobchack stands out with her phenomenologically oriented film theory book *The Address of the Eye: A Phenomenology of Film Experience* (Princeton, 1992). And I could mention the long series of seminars, workshops, and lectures in media programs reaching from Aarhus, Denmark; Bergen and Trondheim, Norway; Goteborg, Sweden; Jena, Germany; Vancouver, Canada, with a recent recognition in the surprise presentation to me of the Walter J. Ong Award by the Media Ecology Association (2010). Locally, there has also been a long, collaborative history with E. Ann Kaplan at Stony Brook's Humanities Institute with the two of us occasionally offering seminars on media related topics. And while these examples of unexpected and unpredicted audiences are not exhaustive, it is an indication of the role of multistability in an experimental phenomenology, which expanded over time and through different disciplines.

I want now to take a third and last, retrospective glance at the history of experimental phenomenology. As noted above, the third mid-career book, *Technics and Praxis*, marked my turn, first to philosophy of technology, later to what was to become *technoscience studies* and through this trajectory, phe-nomenology in its experimental and variational mode takes a *material turn*. One of the early critical responses to *Experimental Phenomenology* was that by choosing abstract, ambiguous drawings as the subject matter, some wondered if perhaps I was avoiding the more complex, "real world" issues that are the harder problems for philosophy. I am hopeful the new chapters added to this second edition will remedy this impression. Here, again, the move to Stony

Brook was crucial: as a research university that allowed for and insisted upon more research, but also as a university dominated by the natural sciences, there was a different environment from which to do philosophy. Already in *Technics and Praxis*, I had begun my material turn—I argued that the sciences *are materially embodied in their technologies*, and the case examples I worked out were a phenomenology of instrument use. (I had also followed Heidegger in his insistence that modern technology was ontologically prior to modern science.) Many technologies, instruments in particular, occupied a *mediating position* in the interrelation between humans and their lifeworld. Compared to the exampleset in *Experimental Phenomenology*, here technologies within intentionality were complex, materialized phenomena. This work took specific shape in the mid-'80s. Earlier I had recognized, of course, that if I followed Husserl's method of variations, including his overly complex "reductions," I should find "essences"—but I didn't. Instead, I discovered multistabilties. By doing phenomenology in practice, I was finding a different result than in its classical expression.

This era of the '80s saw a cascade of debates which impacted the philosophical scene: there were the "culture wars," the "science wars," "post-modernism" and the questioning of modernism, and the rise of both "social constructionism" and "feminism" in relation to what today is called *technoscience*. In philosophy two of the noisiest controversies related to "realism and anti-realism" in the philosophy of science, which echoed in the context of the science wars, and also the emergence of Richard Rorty's defense of an analytic pragmatism as a *nonfoundational* philosophy. My readings in this environment returned me to themes from my interests in the early-twentieth-century experientialist philosophies of both American pragmatism and European phenomenology. Stimulated by those current debates, I increasingly discovered my latent sympathies precisely for pragmatism, which I was rediscovering had interesting implications for a phenomenological experientialism. I found myself in Goteborg, 1984, doing lectures on a "nonfoundational" phenomenology which incorporated pragmatism's nonfoundationalism and antiessentialism into phenomenology itself. This was clearly not classically "Husserlian." These lectures were later published in Ference Marton's phenomenography series as *Non-Foundational Phenomenology* (Goteborg, 1986). Here, in the new context of the second edition, chapter 10 summarizes this adaptation of pragmatism into phenomenology on its way to *postphenomenology*. Of course I had already rejected the transcendental version of phenomenology in the first edition, and sided more with the existential and hermeneutic strands. And the antiessentialism, associated both with transcendental philosophies, was also implicitly nonfoundational. So, now if one adds a material turn, the question arises about the role multistability would take materially. My own first answer took shape in *Technology and the Lifeworld* (Indiana, 1990), which was a systematic and more fully worked out philosophy of the technological lifeworld following the earlier *Technics and Praxis*. In *Technology and the Lifeworld* I worked out a very complex comparison of two cultural practices, which involved technologies, hermeneutic strategies, and different roles for embodied perceptions. The foci were European compared to South Pacific navigational systems, both of which accomplished their praxical roles, but in radically different ways. Here was an example of a material-cultural multistability (I did not include this example here.)

Shortly thereafter, realizing that "nonfoundational phenomenology" was a clumsy term, in a collection of essays relating to the era's concerns with postmodernism, I rephrased the style of phenomenology being developed as *postphenomenology* in my *Postphenomenology: Essays in the Postmodern Context* (Northwestern, 1993)—this term has now stuck, and despite criticisms from many traditional, and primarily European quarters, I am happy enough with this designation. A much more complete account of postphenomenology may be found in *Postphenomenology and Technoscience: The Peking University Lectures* (SUNY Press, 2009).

Chapters 11 and 12, both previously presentations at Science Technology Studies (STS) conferences in Europe, the one in Graz, Austria, the other Darmstadt, Germany, return to media. "Simulation and Embodiment," chapter 11, does a phenomenology of early cinema, through audio-video, to simulation technologies with special reference to whole body perception. Chapter 12, "Multistability and Cyberspace," examines multistability particularly in the use of video display screens and the variations upon POVs or points of view common to computer and video games. I have characterized postphenomenology as incorporating certain pragmatist strategies; retaining the rigorous techniques of phenomenological variations, and doing concrete or "empirical turn" case studies as found in contemporary STS and science studies interdisciplines. Chapters 11 and 12 are examples of this phenomenological-empirical turn.

This formation of a postphenomenology I have discussed more fully elsewhere (*Postphenomenology and Technoscience*, 2009), so here I will only note in passing that it was in the context of the technoscience research seminar, which began in 1998, that this style of analysis took shape. During the same time period, my own research interests had more and more focused upon *imaging technologies*, broadly taken, but with a special interest in science imaging. Chapters 13 and 14 are examples of this more recent set of researches. "Variations upon the *Camera Obscura*," chapter 13, emerged from a pattern of more than a decade of work on the history and phenomenology of visualist imaging in the sciences. It was the first long-history example set that demonstrated how variations upon some originally simple technology or instrument, could lead to proliferating trajectories of discovery in precisely the clear patterns earlier noted in phenomenological experimentation. Chapter 14, "The Seventh Machine: Bow-under-Tension," is an even longer historical-phenomenological example of multistability, by looking at bows in three selected trajectories as weaponry, musical instruments, and various tools. Now, as with the first edition, the second edition shows by way of many more material histories and phenomenologies how to engage in an experimental phenomenology become a postphenomenology. This is what a book is supposed to show, but I want, too, to add a postscript as well, because this style of postphenomenology was honed out of the now more than a decade of the Stony Brook technoscience research seminar and its spin-offs.

Beginning in 2006 and continuing today, participants in the seminar—visiting faculty, visiting scholars, doctoral students from several departments—all did research projects following "empirical turn" styled studies such as are common in science studies and STS or science-technology studies. We began to form "postphenomenological research" panels at a number of relevant societies—The Society for Philosophy and Technology, The Society for Phenomenology and the Human Sciences, The Society for the Social Studies of Science—and to date some fifty participants have done presentations with a significant number eventually publishing their papers. And while most of these have undertaken at least short visits to the research seminar, others have worked in their own university contexts and joined our panels. A second locus for postphenomenology revolves around Peter Paul Verbeek, University of Twente, the Netherlands. His group, too, joins those from the technoscience seminar in these programs. These are mostly younger scholars, from Asia, North and South America, and Europe, indeed from roughly fifteen countries to date. This is a kind of research community, constitutes an experimental beginning for philosophy in the contemporary world.

Preface to the First Edition

Like so many philosophical ventures, this book began accidentally. I had just read an article on multistable perception, which had been pointed out to me by a colleague who knew I had been doing some hesitating and preliminary work on ambiguous drawings such as those employed by Maurice Merleau-Ponty and Ludwig Wittgenstein. I thought the article inadequate and sometimes inaccurate. Because I contemplated making a reply to it, I took the issues raised to my phenomenology classes, playing with them and trying out ideas with my students. The result was a happy surprise: the students were able to grasp certain essential ideas in phenomenology through the use of visual examples much more quickly than with any previous approach.

It also became apparent that the students needed a concrete introduction to phenomenology—that is, one that works through examples in a step-by-step fashion without being either boring or too difficult. Thus was born *Experimental Phenomenology*.

The expert in the field will here recognize a Husserlian flavor to this introduction. This is deliberate; while my own sympathies do not ultimately lie with Husserl, I am convinced that phenomenology must begin with his approach, which is more like analytic philosophy than other types of phenomenology. First come rigor and distinction making; then come depth and extrapolation.

I would like to thank a much larger number of persons than I can mention here, first among them, Patrick Heelan, whose stimulating conversation first encouraged me to write on this topic. I would like also to acknowledge the helpful criticisms of my students and colleagues at Stony Brook, the typing and preparation of the manuscript by Lillian Richardson, and the helpful editing and grammatical revision provided by Robin Elliser and Margaret Thomas. I am also continually grateful to my wife and children for their patience and understanding: when writing, I am inclined to be "somewhere else" during conversation or dinner. They, too, have had some share in developing the text. Several of the most imaginative hermeneutic stories were inventions of my children who, better than many older persons, are often able to grasp an essential insight with ease.

Acknowledgments

Of all the editorial assistants I have had, Adam Rosenfeld has now had the most and deepest experience. He has served for this book, but also the second edition of *Listening and Voice* (SUNY, 2007) as well as many other shorter projects. I feel he knows my habits perhaps better than anyone else, and I remain highly grateful for his patience and insight. It would be too much to cite the many, many seminar participants who have also read and critiqued work, but previous doctorates, Evan Selinger, Ken Yip, Robert Rosenberger, and Kyle Whyte, all also long technoscience workers deserve special mention. Bob Crease, Pat Grim, Lorenzo Simpson, Donn Welton, and Eduardo Mendieta have also played major roles with the process., including those of doctoral committees. And Megan Craig, Anne O'Byrne, and Rita Nolan have previously responded to book party events along with some of those previously mentioned. Similarly, Visiting Scholars over so many years should be noted, but again are too many to mention for such a long series of conversations and discussions, and presentations, too. Alissa Betz, our Staff Associate—and my son, Mark, also keep the computers and printing rolling, and Linda tries to keep me in balance in the background as well.

Chapter Acknowledgments

Chapter 10 was originally presented as "Pragmatism + Phenomenology = Postphenomenology" at the Husserl Circle, Dublin, Ireland, 2005, and while copied in the proceedings does not call for permissions. Chapter 11, "Simulation and Embodiment," was presented at the Institute for Advanced Studies on Science and Technology (STS) in 2003 in Graz, Austria. It was published in the *Yearbook of the Advanced Studies in Science and Technology* (Profil Verlag, 2004) and is reprinted here with the permission of the publisher. Chapter 12. "Multistability and Cyberspace," was presented at the conference on

Transforming Spaces: The Topological Turn in Technology Studies, 2002 in Darmstadt, Germany; the abstract is online. Chapters 13 and 14, while based upon some previously used illustrations, articles, and lectures, are new to this edition. Some of the work on the *camera obscura* has been published in another form as "Art Precedes Science: or Did the Camera Obscura Invent Modern Science?" in *Instruments in Art and Science*, Vol. 2, ed. H. Schramm, L. Schwarte, and J. Lazardzig (Berlin: Walter de Gruyter, 2008) and variations on the archery trajectory are included in my *Postphenomenology and Technoscience: The Peking Lectures* (SUNY, 2009). In both cases, while the illustrations are repeated, the text is not.

Illustrations Acknowledgments

Drawings of the Necker Cube, Projections of a Cube and of a Depth Reversal of a Real Object are from "Multistability in Perception," by Fred Attneave. Copyright © (December 1971) by Scientific American, Inc. Reprinted with permission, all rights reserved.

Imagining: A Phenomenological Study, by Edward S. Casey. Copyright © 1976 by Indiana University Press. Reprinted by permission of the publisher.

The Social Construction of Reality: A Treatise in the Sociology of Knowledge, by Peter L. Berger and Thomas Luckmann. Copyright © 1966 by Peter L. Berger and Thomas Luckmann. Reprinted by permission of Doubleday and Company, Inc.

"The Experience of Technology: A Phenomenology of Human-Machine Relations" by Don Ihde. Copyright © 1974 *Cultural Hermeneutics*. Reprinted by permission of the author.

The illustrations from chapter 10 following are all drawn or redrawn by Don Ihde, with the exceptions of the *camera obscura* series, 13.2 through 13.5 in chapter 13. This series was drawn by Max Liberon, a talented Stony Brook MFA graduate who participated in the technoscience research seminar and did the drawings for Don Ihde's imaging research.

Part I

Experimental Phenomenology

An Introduction

1

Introduction

Doing Phenomenology

Many disciplines are better learned by entering into the doing than by mere abstract study. This is often the case with the most abstract as well as the seemingly more practical disciplines. For example, within the philosophical disciplines, logic must be learned through the use of examples and actual problem solving. Only after some time and struggle does the student begin to develop the insights and intuitions that enable him to see the centrality and relevance of this mode of thinking. This learning by doing is essential in many of the sciences. The laboratory provides the context within which one learns to see according to a scientific modality. Gradually the messy blob of frog's innards begins to take the recognizable shape of well-defined organs, blood vessels, and the like. Similarly, only after a good deal of observation do the sparks in the bubble chamber become recognizable as the specific movements of identifiable particles.

In philosophy also, this learning by example and experience is an important element—but learning by doing is more important in some types of philosophy than in other types. For example, in the two dominant contemporary styles of philosophy, analytic and phenomenological, doing either an analysis or a description calls for putting into practice a certain method of inquiry. But in the case of phenomenology, I would make an even stronger claim: *Without doing phenomenology, it may be practically impossible to understand phenomenology,* This is not to say that one may not learn *about* phenomenology by other means. Certainly, much can be learned about the history, the structure of the inquiry, the methodological presuppositions of phenomenology (or any type of philosophy) by a careful reading of major thinkers, secondary writers, and criticism. In fact, learning the background and establishing the context is not only usual for learning a philosophical style, it is an essential element of a comprehensive grasp of the discipline. Nevertheless, without entering into the *doing,* the basic thrust and import of phenomenology is likely to be misunderstood at the least or missed at most. Phenomenology, in the first instance, is like an investigative science, an essential component of which is experiment. Phenomenology is *experimental* and its experiments are conducted according to a carefully worked out set of controls and methods. It is this dimension of phenomenology that this book addresses. The thought-experiments—or better, experience-experiments—that are worked out here are attempts to show the way in which phenomenological inquiry proceeds.

Most academic settings have ample resources for supplementary reading in the form of primary texts, anthologies, and interpretations.[1] I would recommend particularly readings in the works of Edmund Husserl, Martin Heidegger and Maurice Merleau-Ponty.[2] The difficulty with these texts is that they present the beginner with accomplished results, often in a language that is, at first, quite difficult to penetrate. Such books are not self-explanatory. They often presuppose a good deal of philosophical sophistication in general and some minimal familiarity with at least one particular tradition within philosophy (the transcendental tradition). Moreover, even with this background, the originators of the phenomenological style of philosophy themselves had a difficulty in moving from purely textual acquaintance with phenomenology to its import as a means of investigation. Martin Heidegger (clearly, one of the giants of the phenomenological movement) confessed that although he had thoroughly read the main works of Edmund Husserl (the primary "inventor" of phenomenology), he was not able to understand the full sense of phenomenology until he learned to "see phenomenologically."

> My repeated beginning also remained unsatisfactory, because I couldn't get over a main difficulty. It concerned the simple question how thinking's manner of procedure which called itself "phenomenology" was to be carried out. . . . My perplexity decreased slowly, my confusion dissolved laboriously, only after I met Husserl personally in his workshop. . . . Husserl's teaching took place in a step-by-step training in phenomenological "seeing" which at the same time demanded that one relinquish the untested use of philosophical knowledge. . . . I myself practiced phenomenological seeing, teaching and learning in Husserl's proximity after 1919.[3]

This has been a common experience of those who have learned to do and appreciate phenomenology.

This book aims to overcome some of the difficulties attendant on first learning phenomenology by stressing from the outset the doing, the actual practice of a phenomenological descriptive analysis. The methods of phenomenology will be shown by way of undertaking a special set of inquiries. Phenomenology is to be taught here by way of experiment. But at the same time, it is my hope that the reader will grasp some of the excitement and implication of phenomenology for philosophy and other disciplines.

Of course, no inquiry begins in a vacuum. Even a relatively unfamiliar method or type of thought must make at least minimal contact with previous or extant thought. This is no less the case with phenomenology than it is with every other type of philosophy. To establish the context, this chapter first addresses the present state of affairs. Phenomenology as a term is currently in the air. One hears it, not only in philosophy, but also with respect to other disciplines. There is (or was) a "phenomenological physics," which has as one of its elements a return to a close look at certain phenomena specifically considered in isolation from current or dominant theories of explanation. There is talk about a "phenomenological psychology" or at least about phenomenological elements in psychology. In this so-called phenomenology, the "subjective experiences" of a subject are made thematic. In the social sciences, current ethnomethodology and the notion of "participant observation" have links to the phenomenological tradition. There is also a "phenomenology of religion," the beginnings of a "phenomenological" literary criticism, a revival of interest in the phenomenological dimensions of logic, and a host of other new, but as yet undeveloped incursions of phenomenology into other disciplines.

Initially, the current spread of the term *phenomenology,* and the jargon or tribal language that accompanies it, is not necessarily helpful. Mere familiarity with terms often leads to a false sense of security gained from a superficial understanding of their meaning; this superficial understanding floats on the surface of a mind cluttered with the debris of misunderstandings and criticisms arising from these misunderstandings. On the other hand, it is now clearly the case that within philosophy, phenomenology is recognized as a major style of philosophical inquiry. This stands in marked contrast to the philosophical scene only a decade ago. Today most major departments have at least one philosopher who specializes in some version of scholarship directed toward phenomenology, whether as an active proponent, a critic, or a highly interested onlooker. As time goes on, more and more departments are developing subspecialities in phenomenology.

Precisely because phenomenology is still a minority voice of current American philosophy (though it is no longer totally unknown or merely a target of severe criticism), it cannot claim "self-evidence" or have common assumptions regarding even its own knowledge of itself.

A few preliminary glances both at claims made by phenomenologists and at familiar criticisms facing phenomenology, may clarify the context in which an introduction to the subject may properly begin. In what follows, I shall pair claims made by phenomenologists with familiar and widespread criticisms of phenomenology, trying to show, both why certain preliminary criticisms are all but unavoidable and why much of this criticism is not necessarily well-founded. Finally, however, each reader must see for himself or herself, but I hope that judgment will be informed by direct knowledge.

First, phenomenology as a relatively new philosophical method claims to be a *radical* way of thought. Its founder, Edmund Husserl, claimed, "There is only one *radical* self investigation, and it is phenomenological."[4] Martin Heidegger, following Husserl, claimed, "Phenomenology is our way of access to what is to be the theme of ontology, and it is our way of giving it demonstrative precision. *Only as phenomenology, is ontology possible.*"[5] Clearly these are strong claims and ultimately their fulfillment must come only through what may actually be delivered via phenomenology.

But as a radical philosophy, phenomenology necessarily departs from familiar ways of doing things and accepted ways of thinking. It overturns many presuppositions ordinarily taken for granted and seeks to establish a new perspective from which to view things. Whether or not it succeeds in this task remains to be seen, but note what must necessarily be the case if phenomenology *is* a radical philosophy, quite apart from its success or failure.

If a method is genuinely radical and new, then its new concepts and methods will in some degree be unfamiliar and strange—at least at first. The very displacement of the familiar is such that an initial obscurity will result. A new language will flow from the new concepts, or at the very least, new meanings will be given to older terms. In any case, mastery of a particular language will be called for if the philosophy is to be understood. I shall call this "essential obscurity" and shall try to show that such "essential obscurity" is temporary. It belongs to a certain stage of learning.

In a negative form, this characterization of phenomenology is a familiar criticism. It is widely held that phenomenology is obscure and difficult, if not impossible to understand. Here, the reasons for possible obscurity must be clarified. If, at base, phenomenology should turn out to be contradictory within itself; if its fundamental concepts are confused *after* being scrutinized; or if its claims, not on an initial look but after critical examination, are ill-founded; then the criticism is well-founded. But if the criticisms are superficial, the result of insufficient insight or understanding, then the issue is quite different. It is with this possibility in mind that I would like to examine several distinct forms of confusion.

I have already noted that there is an initial "essential obscurity" that necessarily belongs to the first stage of phenomenology. But this type of obscurity may be temporary as well as not unique to phenomenology. It is, rather, the type of obscurity that comes with any genuinely new mode of inquiry. Historically, one may point to many such examples in relation to the history of science. Revolutions in science have been characterized by Thomas Kuhn as "paradigm shifts."[6] These occurrences are shifts in the way things are viewed. Until the view is resettled, until the basis for the new perspective is solidified, there remains an area of possible misunderstanding between those holding to the former paradigm and those holding to the new paradigm; frequently, there may be problems for those within the new paradigm until its lines of sight are sufficiently freed from the past paradigm. It is this genesis of shift and clarification that belongs to what I have called "essential obscurity."

For instance, when Copernicus began to develop his theory of a heliocentric universe in which the sun was the center of the planetary system, most scholars of his time thought such a notion odd, obscure, and even unthinkable. It was a counterintuitive idea in the sense that, what one saw with one's own eyes and what one knew by established theory was the centrality of the earth. The sun rose and set in an observed movement from a fixed earth, which one could experience. These facts were grounded in long-held theories. What was lacking, for our purposes here, was a requisite question: "From what perspective and in what framework can such a departure from common sense become possible?" Copernicus had already projected a new, as yet only imaginary, stance, different from man's ordinary position on the earth. He became as a distant deity watching the earth move around the sun from a position that he, as an earthbound man, had never inhabited nor could have inhabited at that time. To see the glory of the earth from afar has become possible only in our own time—but its abstract possibility was already latent in the revolution of standpoint contained in Copernicus's theory.

Given this shift, what counted as fact was seen differently by those who took the earthbound stance as primary and those who joined the Copernican revolution with its heavenly stance. Thus argument could no longer presume the same grounds.

This new stance opened the way for even further extrapolation, which Copernicus, himself, found difficult to accept. Giordano Bruno, for example, soon made the extrapolation that if a displacement of the earth from its center made a new view possible, it was also possible to displace the sun as well. To leap outward was but a first step; if our solar system could be so viewed, why could not the other stars also be so viewed, and so on infinitely. Thus, the postulation of other planetary systems, multiple suns, and even multiple inhabited worlds in an infinite universe could be posited. The first revolution, which destroyed the earthbound stance, now could be extrapolated to a possible infinity of positions, all equally possible.

Historically, we know that, in spite of resistance, argument, and even persecution, what was previously taken as odd, obscure, and unthinkable became accepted, even taken for granted or obvious as we might say now. It was this struggle for the requisite insight that would make things clear from a wholly new standpoint that created the first "essential obscurity." This obscurity in turn became "intuitive" and could later be seen as a temporary obscurity.

The implicit claim here is that, if phenomenology is indeed a new modality of thought, the source of its obscurity is only a temporary or "essential obscurity," which necessarily belongs to the new. Once the point of view that makes its view of things possible is made clear, its language and meaning yield their own clarity.

But there is a second and somewhat more superficial obscurity which can accompany the first. This obscurity is the initial obscurity that accompanies all theoretical and technical disciplines. When one first learns a discipline, one also must learn a "tribal language." In philosophy, those who read Kant for the first time, or Leibniz, or even Nietzsche, may find words being used in a different and often technical way. Philosophy rarely reads like fiction, and at first, many people have to read texts phrase by phrase in order to comprehend them. One first approximates the internal meaning or, as Merleau-Ponty points out, one "sings" the language before one clearly understands it.[7] This type of obscurity is also temporary; it calls only for a serious attempt at entering the new language. Phenomenology's tribal language contains a whole vocabulary of technical terms: "intentionality," *epoché*, "the phenomenological reductions," "being-in-the-world," and the like, while quite familiar to the tribe of phenomenologists, remain opaque to the other tribes of the world. But if a discipline is to be mastered, the technical language simply must be learned. That is as true of sciences, logic, alternate styles of philosophy as it is of phenomenology.

A third kind of obscurity sometimes occurs that is to be deplored. Essentially, this consists of the language some phenomenologists, particularly commentators and imitators, introduce by inserting unnecessary obscurity and even cuteness into their language. Whatever the motive, any attempt to cover confusion or pretend profundity by means of excess verbiage is naturally distasteful.

Finally, there is the possibility of a *fundamental* obscurity. Such an obscurity reveals fundamental inconsistency, confusion, or a final lack of plausibility. This obscurity can be discovered *only* by careful analysis and rarely appears on the surface. In philosophical history, such deep obscurity has nearly always been discovered only after great effort and time, usually by surpassing the philosophy being criticized. But surpassing a philosophy entails learning its lessons, and so, no revolution in thought is total.

Thus, the claim here is not that phenomenology will be shown to be without possible flaw or limitation. The claim is, rather, that most presumed obscurity will be shown to be of the temporary variety; once its stance is properly appreciated, its own clarity can and will emerge.

The second claim made by phenomenologists is that at its first stage, phenomenology has developed a genuine "science of experience," which Husserl earlier called a rigorous "descriptive psychology." This *phenomenological* psychology is quite different from most extant psychologies, as I shall attempt to show in the body of this book, although the examples are limited primarily to perceptual examples.

Paired with this second claim is a widespread objection to phenomenology which takes the form of accusing phenomenology of being "subjectivistic" and, at its extreme, accuses it of being a reversion to nineteenth-century introspective psychology. Critics of this persuasion intimate that this subjectivity is bad and unworthy both of philosophy, which must be distinct from psychology, and of psychology, which in much of its current phase avoids the question of so-called subjective states. Everyone, of course, would not consider the examination of experience or introspection to be bad. But the question is not really whether phenomenology examines experience, but *how* it does, and with what method and result.

That phenomenology claims to have developed a genuine "science of experience" despite the objections of those who are suspicious of subjectivity calls for a prolonged examination of what phenomenology studies and how phenomenology interprets experience. In terms of its earlier development, phenomenology claims to examine human experience and to be a rigorous science of experience. This inextricably involves psychological questions.

However, confused with the issue concerning psychology is an issue of strictly philosophical import concerning theories of evidence. At stake is a radically different framework within which the question of what shall count as evidence takes its place. As a preliminary, it can be stated that phenomenology demands that its evidence must be "intuitable," which means, in its proper context, that what is given or accepted as evidence must be actually experienceable within the limits of and related to the human experiencer. But, as will be shown later, this notion is a highly complex one and must be qualified to such an extent that what is ordinarily taken as experience itself undergoes significant change.

Precisely because phenomenology directs its first glance upon experience, it necessarily employs some form of reflection, and in part this reflection must include what has heretofore been known as introspective data. However, there are serious misunderstandings of what has been meant by introspection, particularly as it is transformed in a phenomenological account. Yet, insofar as so-called introspective data are relevant to a comprehensive account of experience, they must be included. What cannot be admitted is that introspection is *the* method of phenomenology.

The confusion between what shall count as psychology and what shall count as philosophy arose at the beginning of phenomenology, and in part must be attributed to the language employed by Edmund Husserl. Husserl's use of language made such objections all but inevitable. The terms *ego, consciousness, subjective states,* and *transcendental subjectivity* cannot help but lead the casual reader to the conclusion that phenomenology is a type of psychology. What the casual reader misses is the transformation of meaning that occurs in terms within phenomenology from Husserl on.

This linguistic confusion belongs to the general problem of introducing a new mode of thought within an already known language, in this case, the language of modern philosophy with its notion of "subject" and "object." For a new thought to be expressed, it must either introduce a radically new language—at the risk of not being understood at all—or stretch the meanings of previous terms to cover new uses. In its history phenomenology has done both, but for the most part Husserl took already well-used terms and gave them special meanings. The result, however, is that one must read carefully and critically to detect the new meanings he sought to establish, meanings often contrary to the traditional ones. Compounding this situation, Husserl's published works lack carefully worked-out concrete examples that would have clarified this heuristic use of language.

To counter the accusation of subjectivism, phenomenologists have tried to draw a sharp line between what has ordinarily been known as introspection and what is developed phenomenologically as "reflexivity." Although the distinction will be developed more thoroughly in subsequent chapters, it is important initially to note that introspection is, roughly speaking, the straightforward taking of subjective data, usually interpreted as "directly present to the mind." This notion of direct presence belongs to both the rationalist and empiricist traditions in philosophy and finds its theoretical context in what phenomenologists call Cartesianism. These traditions locate subjective phenomena "within" a subject and contrast these phenomena with objective phenomena located "outside" the subject. Furthermore, it was Modern Philosophy that brought into fullest and sharpest usage the terms *subject, ego, material bodies,* etc.—the very language that Husserl at first adopted.

Initially, phenomenology transforms the Modern tradition by taking two steps. First, what was previously regarded as "present to the mind" is taken within phenomenology as a genuine field of possible data: phenomena. This field, however, needs to be fully discriminated and clarified; that task constitutes one part of phenomenological inquiry. This being so, all phenomena as "present to a subject" may be regarded as worthy of investigation. Images, percepts, moods, arithmetical phenomena, or whatever may be a valid region for inquiry. It is in this sense, and in this sense only, that so-called introspective data may be considered. But it should also be pointed out that *extrospective* data are equally to be considered. What is investigated, is the field of phenomena.

But within phenomenology, phenomena are never taken as self-evident nor are they inevitably interpreted as "within the mind." Both introspective and extrospective phenomena must be located more precisely within the phenomenological analysis, and it is at this point that the distinction between "introspection" and "reflexivity" comes into play. For phenomenology, the central feature of experience is a *structure* called "intentionality," which correlates all things experienced with the mode of experience to which the experience is referred. The full meaning of this notion will be explained at length in the next chapter. Here, it is only important to note that, far from being self-evident or initially transparent, the "subject" is enigmatic for phenomenology. It is known only *reflexively* from which phenomena and how these phenomena are made present to it. "Introspection," in its Cartesian sense, is taken by phenomenologists to be a naive notion open to the same degree of suspicion in which subjectivism is held. But at the same time, phenomenology does not simply revert to a reductionistic strategy which discards phenomena together with the problems concerning access to phenomena.

In order to set the context, I have taken two initial claims of phenomenologists and paired them with two widespread objections to phenomenology. It should now be apparent that another preliminary task is to introduce at least a minimal vocabulary and set of concepts so that the experiments can get underway. This book will proceed by establishing certain elementary phenomenological distinctions and terms, putting these in as clear a fashion as possible by means of concrete demonstrated examples.

What an elementary—though not to say easy—introduction to phenomenology must accomplish, if it is to be successful, is a restatement of the main themes, ideas, and directions of a style of thought in a language that has been given a clear and illustrated rationale. Simplicity, here, will mean a step-by-step procedure with particular regard to the main terms and concepts of phenomenology. I will introduce the basic vocabulary of the tribal language, but will often put explanations in my own language in order to show the basic sense of the phenomenological method.

Simplicity will require following a process of investigation, since this book is intended as an introduction to phenomenology through experiments. Through the examination of concrete problems as opposed to merely programmatic texts, experimental phenomenology attempts to show *how* phenomenology works. Because this method makes an extra demand upon the reader, it is essential that the reading of this text be accompanied by following actual experiential examples. While the language of the text will be as clear and simple as possible, the demand upon the reader will be more complex. He must *see* what is going on, and by that I mean *see* in its most concrete and literal sense.

The method I will use arises out of an actual set of phenomenological investigations that have been conducted over the last few years in relation to certain problems and puzzles concerning visual perception. Although I shall employ examples involving the other senses, the core examples are taken from a set of familiar, traditional, and already much-interpreted visual illusions, reversible figures, and so-called multistable visual objects.

The choice of this set of examples, which will be reinterpreted in phenomenological terms, itself exemplifies one tactic of phenomenological investigation. The use of simple, familiar examples deliberately opens the way to the sense of phenomenology through an "experiential given" (given in the sense of intuitively familiar). For what could be more familiar than these psychological illustrations? They even appear on restaurant placemats as puzzles in which lines that "appear" curved are in "reality" straight, and as two-dimensional cubes that spontaneously reverse themselves before one's eyes. Moreover, visual as opposed to other sensory examples are implicitly taken to be paradigm examples for all perception and knowledge.[8] Seeing is clear and distinct and is the external counterpart to the internal sense of reason that is *in*sight. Finally, these puzzles and illustrations have already been well interpreted by the standard psychologies and the results, for a "naive" observer, are well known and predictable.

My task will be to take a new look at these examples and try to see and to show them in a phenomenological framework. While doing this, I shall attempt to show how and why phenomenology works the way it does. I hope that in this process, some of the radicalism of phenomenology works the way it does. I hope that in this process, some of the radicalism of phenomenology will begin to show itself, so that the beginner not only will be interested in what is going on, but will also probe into further relations and implications for his own discipline. Secondarily, I hope that some of the prejudices and misunderstandings about phenomenology will either be eliminated or compensated for in a more lucid manner. It is my contention that in its essence, phenomenology is neither obscure nor esoteric and that it holds important implications for a whole range of disciplines.

For the serious student of philosophy, I hope that an introduction by way of phenomenological experimentation will kindle a small sense of excitement for a style of philosophy that does not leave things the way they are, but seeks to make discoveries of its own. A phenomenological analysis (or description, as it is technically called) is more than mere analysis. It is a probing for what is genuinely discoverable and potentially there, but not often seen. Phenomenology is the door to the possible, a possible that can be experienced and verified through the procedures that are, in fact, the stuff of experimental phenomenology.

2

Indians and the Elephant

Phenomena and the Phenomenological Reductions

To get off the ground, a philosophy must choose that with which it begins. At the same time, if it is ultimately to claim to be comprehensive, this choice must be one that potentially includes all that may be needed for universality. Phenomenology, tautologically the study of phenomena, makes this claim as well. The maxim Edmund Husserl coined to characterize phenomenology was, "To the things themselves!"[1] Martin Heidegger, elaborating upon this maxim, noted, "[T]he expression '*phenomena*' signifies *that which shows itself in itself*, the manifest."[2] And, echoing Husserl's call for radicalism in thought, he continued, "Thus the term 'phenomenology' expresses a maxim which can be formulated as 'To the things themselves!' It is opposed to all free-floating constructions and accidental findings; it is opposed to those pseudoproblems that parade themselves as 'problems,' often for generations at a time."[3] But the question is, "How do we properly get to the phenomena themselves?" There is a circle here, which may first be posed in Augustinian fashion: In order to find out, I must in some sense already know; but in order to know, I must find out.

Perhaps a hoary fable can set the tone. Recall the fable of the blind Indians and the elephant, in which a number of feelers-of-elephants were given the task of deciding what the elephant "really" is. The first blind man felt the tail of the beast and related that the elephant was really like a snake, long and sinuous; the second, felt the elephant's leg and related that the elephant was really like a tree trunk, rough and sturdy, etc.

I suppose the fable is meant to make the valid point that parts should not be taken for the whole—but judged by phenomenological standards, these particular blind men are worse off than that. In the first place, in spite of their limited access to the "phenomenon-elephant," the blind men do have

15

"the thing itself" before them. But yet from the outset they miss what may be gained. They do not examine even the limited experience they have with sufficient precision or depth. To feel the hairy, coarse, and knotty-boned tail of the elephant is very unlike grasping the smooth, scaly, and not slimy body of a snake. Nor is the horizontally folded and relatively pliable leg skin of the elephant much like the usually vertically lined and rigid bark of a tree. From the outset, their descriptions are sloppy and based primarily upon simile and traditional beliefs rather than upon a careful analysis of the *phenomenon* before them.

Secondly, they show a tendency typical of an easy or fast "philosophy," that is, they choose to define the reality of the elephant far too quickly, not only prior to examining the whole, but even prior to a careful descriptive analysis of its parts. Leaping to a premature definition prevents the fullness of the "phenomenon-elephant" from being discovered. Instead, it is masked by superficiality.

From the fable, and, more particularly, from the partial phenomenological critique of the fable, it can be seen that a certain initial weighting occurs in phenomenology. This has been characterized as radically empirical, at least in the sense that what is first dealt with is what is taken to be the experience. Such a radically empirical beginning, while not lacking a definitional dimension, stands in contrast to other initial choices of theory, for example, an axiomatic-constructive theory.

An axiomatic-constructive theory begins with a series of definitions and formal relations prior to investigation. Formal systems such as mathematics, logic, and some theoretical sciences begin with a preset language and set of definitions. In such systems, clarity is a function of the definition, and what is "intuitive" refers to logical transparency. A system that begins thus must pay a price for its choice. Often the price is that, that which is not stipulated may not fall within the definition. This excludes certain phenomena on the one hand, while on the other, phenomena within the definition may be left hanging abstractly, as it were, merely contained.

In contrast, phenomenology begins with a kind of empirical observation directed at the whole field of possible experiential phenomena. Initially, it attempts to see things in a particularly open way that is analogous to Copernicus's *new* vision of the universe. Ideally, this stance tries to create an *opening* of a particular type toward things; it wishes to recapture the original sense of wonder which Aristotle claimed was the originating motive for philosophy. Thus, its first methodological moves seek to circumvent certain kinds of predefinition.

A price must be paid for this choice: definitions, if arrived at at all, come quite late, subjecting the initial language of phenomenology to later revision and change as the inquiry progresses. Its benefit is that this initial openness allows the field of inquiry to be wide and relatively free of structure. Such a beginning may appear paradoxical. The paradox consists in the fact that without some—at least general—idea of what and how one is to look at a thing, how can anything be seen? Yet, if what is to be seen is to be seen without prejudice or preconception, how can it be circumscribed by definition? This is one way of stating what is known in phenomenology as a hermeneutic circle, but which I shall call here a *dialectic of interpretation*.

This dialectic of interpretation generates a distance between the axiomatic and the observational in such a way that a direction of inquiry may be taken. The direction first taken is toward the "things themselves," that is, the phenomena present to experience. In this respect, what I shall call the observational side gets a primary weight. Careful looking precedes classification and systematization, and systematization and classification are made to follow what the phenomenon shows.

I want to emphasize, however, that this is an initial weighting and direction, a beginning—not an end, although the beginning determines how any end is to be achieved. A genuinely radical empiricism may, after all, find that things are not at all as they first seemed. This weighting which demands that we first look carefully at what is experienced, and how it is experienced, must be more precisely specified. In what follows, I have for the most part made a somewhat simplified adaptation of Husserlian language and methodology.

The first steps of phenomenological looking are usually called an *epoché*, which means to suspend or step back from our ordinary ways of looking, to set aside our usual assumptions regarding things. Within this general stance, particular levels of stepping back are then determined; these levels are termed *phenomenological reductions*. I shall interpret these specifications as working rules or directions for the way the investigation may proceed. Thus, *epoché* and *phenomenological reductions* may also be called *hermeneutic rules*, since they provide the shape or focus of the inquiry. Hermeneutic in its broadest sense means interpretation, and rules give shape to an interpretation.

The first question is directed to the region of inquiry. What are we to investigate? The motto "to the things themselves" indicates an infinitely open field, including all and any phenomena whatsoever—but only as they are given to experience. Our attention to things that are *given* to experience is with the proviso that we attend to them only as given. This means that we can attend to all the usual furniture of experience, including those prosaic items that philosophers call material objects: chairs, tables, inkstands, and the like. But these objects are to be attended to solely as occurring within experience.

Although this specification may seem too broad to be useful, underneath, we can discern a concentration upon a certain type of inquiry. Our attention is only to those objects that *appear* within experience and we attend only to how they appear. What seems confusing at first is that given objects of experience may not only be many—tables, chairs, inkstands, *ad infinitum*—but any one object of experience may appear in different ways—perceived through the senses, imagined, remembered, hypothesized, etc. Yet this is precisely the first point: the whole of experience may be thus surveyed in its infinite field, as Husserl contended, and the first steps are steps that begin to realize the complexity and immensity of that field.

There is also a second point lurking within the first weighted direction of inquiry. What is sought is what is given; what is sought is what is *immediate* or *present to* the experiencer. Such phenomena as "appearances" are certain, or *apodictic,* as the tribal language puts it. Apodictic here means simply that that which is present, is present in such a way that it shows itself as certainly present. What is immediate or apodictic, however, is also strictly limited to its present givenness. Thus, while it may or may not be the case that the dark shadowy figure I perceive in the hallway really is a person rather than a hatrack, at the moment of the shadow-presentation, I cannot doubt that the presentation is given as I see it, within the limits of the moment of perception.

For philosophers, this very first step is already fraught with latent secondary questions which will ultimately have to be clarified. For example, isn't there a difference between what is "really" the case and what only "appears" to be the case? Isn't it necessary to decide what is sufficient evidence of identity, and only then decide whether the shadowy figure is either a person or a hatrack? Isn't present immediacy illusory and undependable as a basis of knowledge? However, all of these questions, while relevant and important, must be suspended, at first, if phenomenology is to be entered at all. There are phenomenological answers to each of the questions, justifications as affirmative as traditional philosophies would offer, but each answer takes a longer route to explain why such and such must be the case. Thus, if phenomenology is not to founder at the very first step, it is essential that ordinary belief and taken-for-granted theory be suspended so far as to allow glimpses of what will later be seen more fully. Phenomenology calls on us to pretend that what we have as primary, as first given, are these immediate experiences, and to look carefully at them, perhaps more carefully than ever before.

The first operational rule, then, is to attend to the phenomena of experience as they appear. A parallel rule, which makes attention more rigorous, may be stated in Wittgensteinian form: *Describe, don't explain.* This, too, sounds terribly simple, in fact so simple that until it is applied radically, it seems quite trivial. But this seemingly simple rule hides a great amount of complexity, because here, description is meant in a very specific and rigorous way. To *describe* phenomena phenomenologically, rather than *explain* them, amounts to selecting a domain for inclusion and a domain for exclusion. This is a rule that begins to specify the initial goals for phenomenology.

What is excluded is explanation—but what is explanation? In an initial sense, explanation is any sort of theory, idea, concept, or construction that attempts to go *behind* phenomena, to give the reason for a phenomenon, or account for it in terms other than what appears. Again, this seems terribly simple until it is actually tried. Let us look at a set of unexpanded initial examples to show the confusions that may arise from the deceptively simple rule of description.

Imagine a classroom in which the teacher asks the students a series of questions about colors. He asks the class, "Is black a color?" Several hands go up; several answers are forthcoming. The first student says, "Yes, it's the opposite of white." A second student says, "No, black is the absence of all colors," and a third student says, "Black is not a physical color, it is not a color really, it just seems to be a color." What, really, is the case? The answer is long and complex and involves what are known as metaphysical commitments. But now, suppose the teacher points at the chalk board and asks, "What color is that?" In this case the answer will probably be unanimous: "Black."

This example is already quite complex, in that the two questions are quite different in terms of the context they set. In the first question, "Is black a color?" the temptation to give a metaphysical answer is intrinsic. What *really* is the case? With the second question, "What color is that?" the context is confined to ordinary immediacy; ordinary experience is the best judge of the answer. But the metaphysical answer to the first question offers an explanation rather than a description. The type of explanation offered probably depends upon what the students have learned about color from science classes. Ultimately, experienced colors are roughly effects of certain wave lengths of light (such as those that result from the breaking up of white light by a prism) and thus are in themselves "really" not what we see at all. This answer goes behind an apparent phenomenon and explains it by something that is not itself experienced, namely, the wave lengths of light. In its initial—and I stress initial—phase, phenomenology eliminates any such explanation from its descriptions in order to establish a field of purely present experience.

In some measure this helps create clearer boundaries about what will be discussed. A similar move in analytic philosophies would be delimiting various categories of discourse. For example, if I were to ask, pointing to the ladybug crawling across my table, "What do you see there?" and I were to get an answer, "I see red and black stimuli on my retina," not only would I be confused, but I might also say that the answer was a confusion between an explanation and a reported experience.

Now it might seem that phenomenology not only limits itself to appearances, but further limits itself to the realm of ordinary experience, since in each of the above cases, the ordinary-experience answer was approximate to a phenomenological answer. But this is deceptive: the explanatory answers in the above illustrations may also be said to be ordinary, in that they rely upon widely taken for granted knowledge, but even ordinary-experience-contexted answers remain insufficient for phenomenological rigor. What is important to note at this juncture is that one must carefully delimit the field of experience in such a way that the focus is upon describable experience *as* it shows itself. The difficulty to avoid here is a confusion of immediacy with nonexperienced elements presumed or posited in explanations.

The philosophically inclined may be disturbed by this second step. Does this mean that all explanation is to be given up? Does this mean that phenomenology is restricted to ordinary experience? Does it mean that phenomenology is antiscientific, since much science is precisely explanatory rather than descriptive? Again, there are phenomenologically generated answers to each of these questions. But still, the entry into phenomenology in action must be given priority over dealing with each and every objection. Therefore, I shall continue to elaborate initial hermeneutic rules.

The third hermeneutic rule may be stated as *horizontalize or equalize all immediate phenomena*. Negatively put, do not assume an initial hierarchy of "realities." In its original form, this part of the phenomenological reductions called for a "suspension of belief" in all existence predicates or beliefs. For obvious reasons, this was one of the hardest of the phenomenological rules of procedure to accept. It was thought to mean that one had to lay aside one's belief in reality itself in order to do phenomenology. This is a gross misunderstanding of the function of *epoché*, which in phenomenology calls for abstention from certain kinds of belief. *Epoché* requires that looking precede judgment and that judgment of what is "real" or "most real" be suspended until all the evidence (or at least sufficient evidence) is in.

This rule is a critical element of phenomenology and must not be skipped over. It may perhaps be more easily understood if it is seen in terms of its *functions*. First, it functions as an extension of an inclusionary/exclusionary rule of description. Included are all phenomena of experience. Excluded are metaphysical and reality judgments as such. These are suspended. But the rationale for exclusion remains strictly in keeping with the first two rules, which require taking careful note of phenomena without either imposing something upon them or too soon concluding something about them. I have stated this hermeneutic rule more positively by calling for the horizontalization of all phenomena at the onset.

By horizontalization, I mean that initially all phenomena must be thought of as "equally real" *within the limits of their givenness*. This procedure prevents one from deciding too quickly that some things are more real or fundamental than other things. An illustration will show what is involved. I turn to conflicting reality beliefs to show how beliefs tend to reduce or distort the full range of appearances, which is the first essential of phenomenological viewing.

Imagine two seers, a "cartesian" seer and a "druidic" seer. Both are assigned the task of observing a series of tree-appearances under a set of varying conditions and reporting what the tree "really" is like. The cartesian seer returns with a very accurate description of the tree's color, the shape of its leaves, the texture of its bark and its characteristic overall shape. However, upon questioning him, we find that out of the conditions under which the tree appearances occurred, the cartesian seer chose as *normative* only appearances in the bright sun on a clear day. His clear and distinct tree, characterized as essentially an extended, shaped, colored configuration, is a cartesian tree, which appears best in the light of day, all other conditions being dismissed as less than ideal for observation.

The druidic seer returns with a quite different description. His tree emerges from an overwhelming nearness of presence and is eerie, bespeaking its druid or spirit within. It waves and beckons, moans and groans, advances and retreats. Upon interrogation, it turns out that his *normative* conditions were misty nights and windy mornings in the half-light of dawn, when the tree appeared as a vague shape emerging from the fog or a writhing form in the wind. His tree is a druidic tree; a quiet sunny day fails to reveal the inner tree-reality.

We now have to reconcile the seers, for neither of their arguments will convince the other of what the tree is "really" like. Phenomenologically we discern that the normative appearance conditions that govern what is taken as seeing are very intricately involved with two sets of reality assumptions about trees and their nature. The cartesian seer believes that reality is clear, distinct, extended, colored, and shaped. Appearances disproving this belief are ranked as distorted, befogged, unclear, and are rejected as a deficient mode of seeing. The druidic seer holds that appearances in bright sunshine mask the true animated reality of the tree. Mist, wind, and rain reveal inner meaning, while bright, daylight appearances are rejected as misleading.

This simplified example shows that each seer sees what he already believes is "out there"; his seeing confirms him in his metaphysics. Phenomenology holds that reality belief must be suspended in order to allow the full range of appearances to show themselves. This is the function of horizontalization.

The three closely related rules I have discussed—(1) attend to phenomena as and how they show themselves, (2) describe (don't explain) phenomena, and (3) horizontalize all phenomena initially—tell us something about how a phenomenological investigation must begin at the first level. But they also leave us searching for some criterion of relevance, for if we remain at this point, we can become lost among things. We can describe anything we like ad infinitum. This confusion of complexities has some worth, in that it might rekindle genuine philosophical perplexity, an approximation of Aristotle's wonder. But, in order to pursue that wonder, we need to establish a general sense of procedure before undertaking the first concrete investigation.

These rules specify the field, and in a certain sense, function negatively, in that they eliminate certain methodological choices. With the next set of hermeneutic or interpretative rules, forming a second level of procedures, a more active side of the phenomenological investigation emerges.

At this stage, another choice is made. Husserl calls for phenomenologists to look, not just at particularities, but to delve into *essential features* (essences) of phenomena. I shall also refer to these as *structural* features or *invariants* within phenomena.

This second choice, particularly in Husserlian phenomenology, seems to link phenomenology with many of the older philosophical traditions that are concerned with particularity and universality. Clearly, the tribal term *essence* seems to make that connection. Essence is a term that, in traditional philosophy, sometimes means a general character: that which a number of things have in common. Sometimes it means a universal, in the sense that a certain number of things belong to it, while others do not. And sometimes it means a condition without which a thing would not be what it is. All of these meanings have their place within phenomenology, but other meanings also arise, such as, "inexact essences" which mean that a thing *positively* lacks precise definition, or (better put) its definition *is* its ambiguity. But rather than determining too quickly and narrowly what essence means, one must found its meaning on phenomenological looking itself. The terms *structure* and *invariant features* should neutralize too quick an identification with other traditions. What this hermeneutic device demands is that phenomena be looked at with a particular interest, an interest that seeks out essential or structural features. Thus, the fourth hermeneutic rule is: *Seek out structural or invariant features of the phenomena.* In this, phenomenology retains its similarity with empirical science. It looks for the structures of things that appear in the way in which they appear. Repeated patterns are significant and must be actively probed.

Probing, too, must take on a phenomenological form. The probing activity of investigation is called *variational method*. Husserl's preferred tool was what he called "fantasy" variations. These variations were modeled on familiar logical and mathematical practices. Thus, to solve a problem the phenomenologist must go through all the variations that will lead to an adequate insight or solution. But, as later phenomenologists pointed out, investigations of regions of experience show that there are sometimes significant differences between the various dimensions of experience. Perceptual variations often contrast with imaginative or conceptual variations, though the activity of varying what is investigated is retained. The method to be used in this book relies upon perceptual experience for the most part.

In its simplest form, the use of variations requires obtaining as many *sufficient* examples or variations upon examples as might be necessary to discover the structural features being sought. This device is not unknown to other philosophies and sciences. Empirical investigations always seek out a series of examples prior to generalization, and contemporary philosophies are quite fond of citing paradigm examples and counterexamples to illustrate the certainty or doubtfulness of a philosopher's claim. However, free variations employed in a systematic way are a central methodological feature of all phenomenological investigation.

Two initial forewarnings should accompany an introduction to variational method. First, the variations must genuinely belong together. Each step of the procedure must be completed prior to wider extrapolation. Once an insight is gained through the use of variations, extrapolation becomes easier and easier as more recognized structural features are accumulated. Second and more seriously, it must be recognized that it is extremely difficult to judge the point at which variations are sufficient. (Later on, phenomenological "levels" and the problem of closure which they pose for all genuine phenomenological investigation will be encountered.)

One objective of the variational method parallels that desired in the horizontalization of phenomena. Variations "possibilize" phenomena. Variations thus are devices that seek the invariants in variants and also seek to determine the limits of a phenomenon. Ideally, of course, variations should be infinite, but, fortunately, this is not necessary since a sufficient number of observations usually yields the essential features.

Return to the example of the tree-observers. In contrast to both the cartesian and druidic seers, the user of variational method gives primary value to the full range of possible tree-appearances. He realizes that it is only through a complete series of possible tree-appearances that essential features may be discerned.

In both the lowest level of hermeneutic rules (which specify the field) and the second level of activity rules (which specify what and how something is to be focused upon), phenomenology resembles an empirical science. It is "empirical" in the sense that it is observational in the first instance; it is "scientific" in that its interest is in the structure of a given phenomenon; and it is "psychological" in that its primary field is that which occurs within experience.

So far, I have been discussing *phenomenological reductions*, those methodological devices that clear the field and specify how it is to be approached. However, a more total possibility may also be attained. If phenomenology is to become *philosophical*, it must make a more total claim to significance in its choices. Such a move, again adopting the language of Husserl, is made by elevating all the previous hermeneutic rules to the level of the *transcendental*. Following the older tradition of Immanuel Kant, what is needed is *a condition for the possibility* of the type of phenomena that show themselves within the phenomenological view. This condition must also be an invariant feature of overall experience, the fundamental structure of experience.

Husserl's claim was that *intentionality* was precisely that structure and precisely that feature of experience overall, which make possible the way in which phenomena can and do appear. Intentionality as transcendental is the condition of the possibility for all experience to be shaped in a certain way. To introduce intentionality at this juncture may be premature. But, by anticipating what for phenomenology is *the* shape of experience, there can be gained a glimpse of overall direction. Intentionality summarizes all that has gone before in this initial framework. Intentionality is the directional shape of experience.

I should like to introduce the terminology concerning intentionality in a preliminary and somewhat unusual way. Rather than describing how intentionality is arrived at in the history of phenomenology, I should like to include its *function* as the ultimate hermeneutic rule by which phenomenology operates. It is the rule that specifies the horizon or boundary of phenomenology within which the totality of things may be dealt with. Intentionality *functions* as a correlational rule, and in his later works, Husserl sometimes spoke of intentionality as *correlation-apriori*. An *apriori* is the ground level that founds all other levels; it may also be considered the limit beyond which phenomenology ceases to be itself. Thus, I shall continue to look at the way in which phenomenology functions, now from the point of view of operating according to a *correlational rule*.

This higher-level correlation rule is nothing more than a further explication of what was implicit in the lower-level rules. The correlation-apriori extends fully and universalizes what was latent in the descriptive strategy of the previous procedures. It makes a universal claim, which moves phenomenology from a regional method and claim (descriptive psychology) to a philosophy.

A correlation rule implies a correlation of something with something. Given a field of (possible) experience, the question is, first, what is to be correlated with what and second, how the correlation is to be interpreted. In traditional philosophies, a distinction is usually made between object and the subject that knows the object. Husserl transformed this distinction into a correlation of what is experienced with its mode of being experienced. He termed the correlation itself *intentionality*. He held that such a correlation was, in fact, invariant to experience and that this correlation could be thought of as directed. All experience is experience of ———. This is to say, all experiencing implies something that is experienced, but within this general concept of experience, two poles can be differentiated descriptively. In an ordinary sense, then, if I am to examine a time-span of my experience, I can, according to Husserl, distinguish within this experience, those items, or *things of experience*, that present themselves to me (at this moment, for example, I see the typewriter, my desk top, the pens, papers, and pencils appear on my desk). The *way* in which these things are present to me (for example, the typewriter appears to me as before me, referring itself to the position I occupy in relation to it; its "b" key is sticking because of the humid weather here in the woods, referring me to my feeling of its resistance to touch, etc.). But while these differentiations may be made, they remain strictly relative or *relational* distinctions: *every experiencing has its reference or direction toward what is experienced, and, contrarily, every experienced phenomenon refers to or reflects a mode of experiencing to which it is present.* This is the intentional or correlation apriori of experience taken phenomenologically.

Husserl gave the two sides of this correlation names that have become traditional. For what is experienced, as experienced, he used the term *noema* or noematic correlate, and for the mode of experiencing which is detected reflexively, he used the term *noesis* or noetic correlate. (Noema and noesis, as used here, and in distinction to the highly technical uses later developed by Husserl, refer simply to the two sides of the correlation rule. They are foci within overall experience, or correlational poles.)

This internal correlation within experience may seem trivial and obvious—if I experience at all, I experience something and in some way. But, in order not to fall outside the boundaries being circumscribed for the phenomenological investigation, note that the correlation applies to and is found in all the various types of observation we include under the name of human experience. Thus, perceptually, I may see something—the typewriter before me, feel it as resisting me, particularly the letter "b"—in a certain way. At the same time, I may imaginatively visualize a green bottle fly buzzing before me. This imaginary noema has its own specific character as imagined, and I detect reflectively, that for it to continue its phenomenological presence before me, I must actively renew it imaginatively. Even emotionally (though mood is not a "representation" of something), a certain mood is present to me in that it gives a color or shade to the whole of the immediate context. In each of these situations, a dimension of experience has its directional and referential focus: it is *intentional*.

However, in this preliminary look at phenomenology, I am emphasizing the correlation of noematic and noetic aspects of experience. This correlation may be simplified as the following set of diagrams show. If what is experienced as experienced (the noema) is placed on one side of a correlation, then the mode of its being experienced (noesis) is always strictly parallel to it. One does not, and cannot, occur without the other. This correlation of noema with noesis may be diagrammed:

$$\text{noesis} \rightarrow \text{noema}$$

Here, noema stands for that which is experienced. The arrow indicates that this experience is directed or referential, and its particular shape in the "how" experienced, is indicated by noesis. Within the phenomenological reduction, then, only that which is so correlated is considered.

Judging from ordinary interpretation of experience, the diagram seems incomplete. It might well be granted that there is always that which is experienced, and, even, that which is the mode of experiencing. However, in an ordinary interpretation, one would also expect to find a *bearer* of experience, a subject, the concrete "I" who does the experiencing. Thus, to complete the diagram it seems a third term is needed:

$$(I) \ \text{noesis} \rightarrow \text{noema}$$
(experiencer) experiencing-experienced

The correlation now seems complete: a relation between myself as the experiencer and something that is present as experienced. At the inception of Husserl's work in phenomenology, something like this was developed. The "I" was for Husserl, the *ego* interpreted as the thinking self. In fact, in the midst of what has been called his egological period, Husserl formulated the correlation as:

Ego–cogito–cogitatum

This defines the correlation as the ego (thinking self) thinking what is thought. However, for my purposes, I have placed the "I" in parenthesis, a modification of the original Husserlian form of the correlation, for reasons that will soon become apparent.

If I begin now to take note of my experience, deliberately trying to find the most straightforward experience possible, I may well make a certain discovery. In most of my straightforward experiences, I am certainly not primarily, or even self-consciously, attentive to what is going on in that experience. Instead, I am busy attending to the matter at hand. Thus, if I am chopping wood for the evening fire in Vermont, I am so involved with splitting the wood that I do not notice much of what goes on around me, nor do I think self-consciously about how it is that I am splitting the wood. In fact, if I do turn critical and self-conscious, while my ax is raised to swing, I may miss the log entirely.

But, after the fact, I may note in this simple report that I can distinguish and easily move between what appear to be two variations within experience. Straightforward experience, I could and did characterize: it was actional, involved, immersed in the project of the moment, narrowly focused, and concentrated. My thinking about that experience, also an experience in the general sense, was a *reflection* or a *thematizing* of the straightforward experience. These two modes of experience are familiar and easily alternate in the ongoing affairs of the day.

This apparently simple distinction between straightforward experience and reflective experience can, however, be misleading. In the straightforward experience, I am involved with things; the straightforward experience is "real," while in the reflective experience, I have already stepped outside "real" experience and begun to think *about* experience—perhaps implying that I am in some sense outside or above experience. Phenomenological reporting is done reflectively. Thinking *about* experience presupposes both some form of experience as its subject matter and some kind of distance from that subject matter in order to thematize it. Thus, in some phenomenology, the reflective move is characterized as a move outside or above or distanced from straightforward experience.

This was the way in which Husserl characterized an early phenomenological version of what I shall call the *reflexive move*.[4] Husserl maintained that phenomenological reporting was done in terms of a modification of reflective thinking, a thinking *about* experience that presupposes some other form of experience as its noema, and some kind of distance in order to thematize that experience. Thus, Husserl frequently characterized the reflective stance as outside or above ordinary or straightforward experience. Here, the "I" transcends straightforward experience and was called a "transcendental ego."

Were I to make a diagram of this interpretation following our first correlation, it would appear thus:

Transcendental Ego (I")

↓

Ego (I') noesis → noema

We have here an enigma. On the one hand, the whole correlation is the noema for the transcendental ego (I"). Conversely, the transcendental ego (I") is interpreted as above and outside the correlation. But if the correlation is itself the ultimate structural feature of human experience, then this transcendental move is questionable. On the other hand, there remains a sense in which the transformation of reflection upon experience still retains the correlation structure, in that the transcendental ego is actually only a modification of the ordinary ego (I') and, as transcendental ego, must be correlated with the new noema. This feature might be diagrammed as:

Transcendental Ego (I") noesis → noema

(Ego-noesis-noema theme)

But this reduces the "outside" and "above" of the transcendental ego to the simple (I) noesis-noema correlation, and makes the transcendental interpretation unnecessary.

This excursus merely records part of the history of phenomenology. Almost all Husserl's followers rejected the transcendental interpretation he gave the ego and turned in what has become known as an existential direction.

Transcendental phenomenology gave way to *existential phenomenology*. I, too, shall ultimately follow this direction, but in such a way, I hope, as to be able to justify why this modification of Husserl is called for. What can now be noted is that a certain general shape for overall experience has emerged. Intentionality as the *direction* of experience within its correlation has a limit and a shape.

This field and shape of intentionality might be conceived in a diagram as an ellipse with two foci:

The field of overall experience is indicated by the ellipse. Since every possible experience falls within the ellipse, strictly speaking nothing lies outside it. Within the ellipse (overall experience) there are two related foci (what is experienced and that to which what is experienced refers). The lines of relation indicate the possible modes of experience. Intentionality is the name for the direction and internal shape of experience. Reflection is the means of bringing forth the specifics of that direction and shape.

We need a somewhat finer discrimination of what happens in reflection. I return to straightforward experience. If I consider the most intense experience and if I make a careful description, I note that any usual sense of "I" is not at all thematized—although I cannot say that I am *unaware* of myself in any total sense. In the woodchopping, my primary energy and concentration is focused *almost* totally in the project itself. In such a situation, I say that I am not *self-conscious*, but this is not to say that I am unaware of being-in-a-situation. I might even go on to describe this situation as one in which "I" should be put roughly as "I-am-in-the-ax-directed-toward-the-wood," or, paraphrasing Merleau-Ponty, "I am outside myself in the world of my project."

To say that self-consciousness is reduced to a minimum, that the "I" of such experiences is not thematized or explicit, is not at all to say that such experiences are lacking in awareness or are opaque. Quite to the contrary, in ordinary or mundane life, such experiences can be a vivid example of the most valued type of experience. In reporting in the ordinary mode, I might well recall such occasions as those when "I was most alive . . ." The "I," in such situations, is the "I" that is most thoroughly involved and enters into the project at hand in such a way that its self-consciousness is reduced to a minimum. Yet, I recognize that the intense involvement experienced must be identified with the "I" that I do thematize in my ordinary—and my phenomenological—reflections. However, because the thematization of this "I" comes afterward, it cannot be made the first element or the most obvious element in the descriptive analysis made in reflection.

From this it can be seen why the "I" in the correlational scheme at the straightforward level was placed within parenthesis. The "I," particularly in its thematized form, comes late in the analysis rather than being given as a first. This is to say, the "I" has a certain genesis or recognizable origin in the movements of experience. But let us now retrace the movement from straightforward experience to a reflection upon that experience.

In my description of chopping wood as a straightforward experience, the most dramatic aspect was the involvement with a range of things concentrated into what appeared, reflectively, as a pattern of relationships. While chopping wood, my perceptual attention is concentrated upon the piece of wood to be cut. The piece of wood absorbs my attention and stands out from the entire environment around me. This is not to say that the piece of wood is all that remains within my awareness, but only that it forms the focal core. I may secondarily be aware of the ax and the aim directed through it—but, if I am a skilled woodchopper, this will be barely noticeable. (Conversely, the begin-ner, who is more aware of the ax and is concerned about hitting the wood just right, allows an "ax-awareness" to intrude, so that he may miss the wood entirely or slice at it rather than cut it.) What stands out as "first" and takes preeminence in such performances, is the *terminal* element of the correlation, the noematic terminus. Thus, as shown in the diagram below, the *noema* in the normative, straightforward experience is that which first appears or stands out within the entire field of possible experience. This noematic focal presence in straightforward experience provides a direction for the inquiry. Its initial primacy opens the way for an order to phenomenological description. I note this initial primacy as:

$$\textbf{(I) noesis} \rightarrow \textbf{noema}$$
$$1$$

I can associate a secondary rule with this precedence: begin observation and description with that which "first" appears in straightforward experience; this is the noematic correlate. It is thus "to the things" that phenomenology turns.

But this initial precedence does not abolish the correlation. Whatever is experienced in a straightforward mode may be reflexively related to the mode of experiencing, which is also open to reflective access. In fact, what stands out within straightforward experience is often quite transparently correlated with what I do, with my turning of attention to this or that thing. Some simple variations show this.

I may be concentrating intensely upon something that does not make any obvious demand upon me. Listening to music, I can make the strains of the oboe stand out from the quartet, even though its voice is recessive when compared with that of the French horn. Or I may be attending to something, when suddenly something else forces my attention elsewhere—while I am listening to the oboe against the stronger strains of the horn, suddenly some other listener in the audience stands up and shouts "Boo," and my attention is instantaneously altered to correlate with this surprising phenomenal demand.

In these instances I have emphasized my attention and its changes and variations. In doing this, I have begun to move toward the second or noetic pole of the correlation. Each appearance appears in a certain way, always relationally to my degree and type of attention. This is part of the noetic correlation. This movement from noema toward noesis provides a second step in the order of the analysis. From any noema I can move toward a noesis, and thus the initial primacy of things can lead to its correlated noetic component:

$$\textbf{(I) noesis} \longrightarrow \textbf{noema}$$
$$2 - - - - - 1$$

The analysis begins with *what* appears (noema) and then moves *reflexively* toward its *how* of appearing.

What appears (the strains of the oboe appearing against the background of the quartet) does so in a certain configuration. Essential to how it appears is this standing out as a core phenomenon against the background phenomenon of the quartet. I listen for the oboe, in spite of the horn; I focus in on the oboe. This is my noetic activity, which allows or actively constitutes the condition for the oboe's standing out. But I note this form of the activity only with respect to what is attended to. Its possibilities are revealed by way of the oboe-quartet configuration. Thus, the shape of the noetic possibility is arrived at by way of the noematic possibility. Noesis appears *reflexively*.

There is but one more step to the process. It concerns the "I." How is the "I" "constituted," as Husserlian language would have it? It is constituted as the noetic terminus, the structured bearer of experience. To diagram the "I" within the correlation is now possible:

$$\textbf{(I) noesis} \longrightarrow \textbf{noema}$$
$$3 - 2 - - - - - 1$$

Here, then, is the order for analysis. Analysis moves from that which is experienced toward its reflexive reference in the how of experience, and terminates in the constitution of the "I" as the correlated counterpart of the noema. The "I" is a late arrival in the phenomenological analysis. In this respect, phenomenological analysis is the inverse of introspective analysis. The "I" is arrived at not directly, but by way of reflexivity. An introspective ego or "I" claims direct, immediate and full-blown self-awareness as an initial and given certain. In phenomenology, the "I" appears by means of and through reflection upon the phenomena that in toto are the world. Put in ordinary terms, the phenomenological "I" takes on its significance through its encounter with things, persons, and every type of otherness it may meet.

This may be seen partially in terms of the correlational scheme itself, now that the order of analysis has been settled. The rationale of the order of analysis comes from the analysis of experiences I have been making. A return to the difference between straightforward and reflective experience may show how the order may be interpreted. Reflective reporting, it was noted, presupposed and in some instances was dependent upon, straightforward experience. To reflect is to reflect about something, which is to say, in phenomenological language, that reflection is intentional. Reflection, too, has a directive or "outward" aim toward certain noema: those that are a previous (or even simultaneous) experience. The modification occurring in this type of reflection is not a modification of the correlation; it is a modification of the noema. The Husserlian positing of a "transcendental ego" is unnecessary, at least with respect to one of its undesirable implications.

Were there to be an "I" somehow above and outside the correlation, rather than constituted reflexively within the correlation, phenomenology would revert to a kind of metaphysical stance it wishes to avoid. If intentionality is not something merely subjective, but is the very means of access to the world, then any observer above or outside the correlation must be a philosopher's god, or some form of ideal observer. But this is precisely what the phenomenological reductions must exclude. Furthermore, if the philosopher is the person who is involved in the correlation itself, then access to the ideal observation can be had only within the correlation, intentionally.

Here, I am anticipating the *existential* transformation of phenomenology. Just as Kierkegaard complained that Hegel had proceeded to construct a grand System and then sat down outside it, forgetting that the philosopher was a human being, so the existential transformation of phenomenology maintains that any "ego" must be concrete. But more is involved than that. The existential phenomenological position maintains that the essential insight of phenomenology is lost unless this correlation is strictly maintained.

In the existential version of the reflexive turn, the "I" remains constantly involved with its projects, except that in a reflection upon experience, the involvement is with a previous or different element within overall experience. In the second diagram on page 28, however, the transcendental position of I" has disappeared, and the diagram simply preserves the initial correlation apriori of intentionality. This is to say that reflective experience retains certain characteristics of every straightforward experience. It has its own mode of involvement, in which the "I" of reflective experience is as involved (and as hidden) as the only implicit "I" of straightforward experience. But it remains the case that something has changed, and this is what is remarkable about reflective experience and gives it at least an initial philosophical advantage. Reflective experience can and does thematize and reflect upon other experience, giving a possibility of self-distancing within overall experience. But the way in which self-distancing occurs must not do violence to the original intentional correlation.

The distancing within experience that is self-distancing is an *internal* difference within the correlation. And the reflexive turn derives its shape from the "mirror" of the world as the totality of noematic possibilities. This existential interpretation of intentionality permits a more rigorous maintenance of the insight of the correlation apriori, and founds the stance from which phenomenological inquiry takes its view.

With this framework in mind, one of the puzzles over the initial choice made within phenomenological theory can be put in perspective. From the point of view of ordinary interpretation, itself already containing the sediment of a long tradition of metaphysical belief, a distinction between "reality" and "appearance" is needed to account for occurrences such as mistakes. For example, at the beginning of this chapter, I referred to a perception of a shadowy presence that could have been either a hatrack or a person. How does one decide which is real and which only apparent? The answer may now be seen to require a more probing inquiry, which includes a reformulation of the question itself.

By setting aside the ordinary interpretation and substituting for it an interpretation within the framework of a correlation theory, we see that what counts as evidence, and what counts in how that evidence is obtained, is of utmost importance. The most naive form of objectivist answer will assume a need for a philosopher's god or ideal observer, declaring that the truth of the situation can be seen from "above," from the point of view of an ideal observer who will know what the shadowy shape "really" is. But this will not do on two grounds. First, I, the concrete observer, am not the god; and second, were such a god needed, I would still have to get access to him from the limits of my actual situation. Thus, I would find myself wondering whether he were genuinely reporting a reality or whether he were the evil genius of Modern Philosophy as per Descartes.

In contrast, if the question is reformulated from a phenomenological position, all I can assume is the stance of my actual position vis-à-vis the world. The development of a dependable and viable distinction between "reality" and "appearance" would then have to come out of a further analysis of the experiential context itself. Could it be that experience, insofar as "truth" is attainable, must correct itself? Do not I, as an actual observer, ultimately decide whether the shadowy figure is a hatrack or a man only by further and more adequate observation? Must not the correction of perceptual mistakes ultimately come from perception, just as the correction of logical mistakes comes from further logical inquiry? At least if this is the case, all that it is necessary to presuppose is the limited situation of being human. What is problematic is the clarification of that situation and its genuine possibilities, and this is the direction that a reformulation of questions addressed to preliminary reservations takes.

Up to this point, a very general and necessarily abstract outline has been offered concerning the question of how phenomenology is to approach the first questions of experience. Seen from this point of view, phenomenology is an examination of experience that deals with and is limited by whatever falls within the correlation of experienced-experiencing. It proceeds in a prescribed order, starting from what appears as it appears, and questions retrogressively from the what of appearance to the how of experience and ultimately back to the who of experience. The hermeneutic rules establish a strictly descriptive interpretation of experience, which eschews explanation and all hypothetical constructions relying upon, presupposing, or seeking to establish accounts of experience that go behind or above experience. Although the critical mind may anticipate problems at each juncture, the next task is to begin the initial observations which call for *doing* phenomenology.

3

The Visual Field

First Phenomenological Excursus

Although not all terms have been introduced, it is now possible to begin an excursus into experience. In this chapter, I shall introduce terms pertaining to structures by way of a visual model. However, despite much philosophical and psychological tradition, dealing with vision in isolation is phenomenologically suspect. Thus, a turn to a visual model must itself be attained phenomenologically.

When I first turn to experience, the problem is one of orientation—to what experience? There seems to be so much of it. How do I orient myself amidst what William James called a "blooming, buzzing confusion"? Mindful that the very questions I put to experience determine a direction, I must take account of its very breadth and complexity.

To meet this requirement, I will make a *catalogue* of momentary experience, trying to note as much as possible of what occurs within a short span of experience.

I take this morning as my point of departure and reflect upon my awakening. What first strikes my attention is the sound of rain falling on the roof of my summer cabin. But rain does not fall without significance, and I am immediately aware of its meaning. Since it is raining, pouring the foundations for the larger house will again be delayed. I become aware of my own feelings of frustration. But these two different phenomena do not exhaust the situation. In contrast to the rain and my frustration, I am aware that my wife lies beside me, still asleep, warm and comforting. And in the midst of all this are numerous fleeting events as well. A yellowthroated warbler has just appeared at the window; there are vague stirrings of hunger within my body; there are the sounds of the children making a fire in the stove, etc.

Thus, my first impression of a span of experience is one of vast complexity and multiplicity. It is a Joycean stream of consciousness which would take pages to elaborate fully.

I make a more careful examination of this initial reflection. I note that although a short experience span is immensely complex, not everything stands out equally, or is equally demanding. I note that my awareness tends to flit from one concern to another, sometimes with great rapidity, sometimes slowly. This flow of events has at least a minimal structure or pattern. Its multiplicities range from that which stands out to that which is on the fringe of my consciousness.

Taking this as a clue, I now turn to a typical philosophical device. I return to experience seeking to simplify it, to reduce it to a manageable dimension. Rather than continue with the vastness of global experience, which is clearly primary, I choose to concentrate solely upon what I see, upon visual phenomena. After all, nothing is simpler than this because I am familiar with the tradition of the five separable senses. But immediately, if I remain strictly phenomenological and attend carefully to the full phenomena, I find something difficult in what I thought simple. I find that I cannot attend solely to vision. No matter how hard I try, the world does not appear to me in a single visual dimension. My global awareness refuses to disappear, and even as I am casting my gaze about me, there remains on the fringes of my awareness the felt weightiness of my body on the bed, the smell of smoke now coming from the fire, and the growing concern with breakfast. I do not and cannot simply rid myself of these presences.

Yet, in spite of this, I am able to *concentrate* my attention upon the visual dimension. The other phenomena do not disappear, their recalcitrant presence remains, but they recede to the fringe of awareness. Simplification is approached but not attained. But I discover a pattern. Just as I was able to concentrate upon the oboe within the quartet, upon the flitting pattern of concerns upon awakening, so I can concentrate upon a visual dimension while mindful that this concentration is not exclusive and does not abolish the full range of global presence. Clearly, it is possible to order things in a scale so that some phenomena stand out and others recede.

Again I return to my experiential exercise, now with phenomenology in mind, and I discover that I have not followed the strict order of description. My reflections have been ordinary in that I have mixed noematic and noetic correlates and have taken the "I" for granted. I have not begun the requisite precise analysis. I now begin to break up the experiential elements into their components, taking note first of noematic features within the visual dimension. Whatever "I" language remains should be taken only as the narrative background to the description.

I look upward toward the ceiling. There is a spider on a small web in the corner of the rafter. This spider and its web stand out as a phenomenon. Its appearance is clear and distinct—but not without a context. Its standing out is clearly relative or relational to that against which it stands out, in this case the rafter and the ceiling boards. This relation, already well known to Gestalt psychology (which was a stepchild of early phenomenology), is a figure-ground relation. I seek variations upon this situation. The same pattern is revealed in a series of items I look at: the alarm clock related to its background of nightstand and wall, the hummingbird now at the window against its background of spruce and fir trees. Wherever I turn, that which stands out visually does so against a background and within a context. I begin to sense an invariance to this visual situation.

Pursuing this invariance, I recall a previous example from the classroom. I went to the blackboard and drew the following figure in chalk:

I asked the class what they saw. The first and ordinary response was, of course, "an 'x.'" The answer was, in the ordinary context, quite correct. But then I asked, "Is that *all* you see?" Obviously, the answer had to be "no." Each student saw more than an "x"; he saw an "x" on-a-blackboard, which in turn was on-the-wall, which in turn was surrounded-by-the-floor-and-ceiling, which in turn gave way to certain desks and other students, depending on which came within the observer's field of vision.

Here, a movement is being made, in spite of seeming triviality, toward phenomenological description. Yet what more obvious observation can there be than that "x's," spiders and alarm clocks appear *only* against a background and *only* in relation to that background? Still, this observation is not necessarily obvious *until it is pointed out*. In fact, were we to do constant variations upon this first simple observation and eventually (adequately) conclude that whatever item appears, *appears only as situated within and against a background,* we should already be upon the verge of making one phenomenological philosophical point. Negatively, and in restricted form, it might be put: *There are no things-by-themselves in the realm of visual presence,* positively: *all items that appear do so in relation to a background and in strict relation with that background.*

This observation is the first intimation of a noematic structural *invariant*. Things as individual items show themselves as related to and situated within a *field*. A thing is relationally determined in this way, and the very notion of a thing-by-itself is at least perceptually an abstraction that belies the full perceptual phenomenon.

But there is something else to notice concerning the appearance of the thing situated within its field: certain things stand out, are focally present, have greater perceptual clarity within central vision. These things constitute a *core* within the total visual phenomenon. Here, I continue to speak about what shows itself, without regard to how this showing comes about. Noematically, what is seen is seen as standing out, as situated at the center of vision, as most explicit.

Moreover, the terms *field* and *core* are related. The thing that stands out as the core item within vision does so against the background (field) which is its context. Thus, *core* and *field* are relational or paired terms concerning what I see.

Now I return to what is seen to discern other features of the visual panorama and attempt a further series of variations. This time, I will try to detect other significant shapes in the things that appear.

I look straight ahead at my fingers. Keeping my gaze fixed straight ahead, I move my finger sideways. I note that when it was in front of me its appearance was clear and distinct and that as it moves to the side, the distinctness gradually lessens, although I can still detect it and note that it can still be distinguished from its background. However, at some point, the visual appearance of the finger disappears, not at any sharp or all-at-once point, but by an almost undetected withdrawal. I move my finger in several directions and discover that the same thing happens whether I move it to the right, to the left, above my head, or at my feet.

What is being evidenced here is the well-known phenomenon of the shape of the *visual field*. This field has a shape with a border or *horizon*. (Note that in phenomenology "horizon" means limit, and so cannot be said to expand or be extended, as in ordinary English.) The shape is roundish. Experiments such as this indicate that there are boundaries to the visual panorama. Any visual phenomenon, as present, occurs only inside or within the field that is situated before and only partly around my bodily position. Furthermore, although I do not ordinarily take note of this, the phenomena appearing at the edges of the field are usually vague and barely noticeable (with known exceptions, such as flashing lights or fast motions) and fade off into the indistinct horizon of the field. Finally, I note that the shape of the field never varies, whatever my bodily position in the world. It is always before me and retains the same configuration for me, regardless of which way I turn.

Now it is possible to come to another conclusion concerning differences within the visual field. The field is bounded by, and situated within a horizon, which has a more or less recognizable shape in spite of its indistinct outline. Thus, in addition to core and field, we have a third term: the paired field located within a horizon or *fringe*. This series of relationships is simplified in the following diagram, representing the visual panorama before me within which all visual phenomena appear:

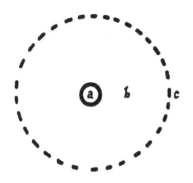

a. = core object in central vision

b. = field or background region surrounding and situating core object

c. = fringe or horizon, which limits and

borders the field of vision

I take note of internal relations within the visual field and discern that graded differences occur in ordinary seeing. First, I note as before, that what appears most clearly is at the core of the field and is centrally located, and that those phenomena located nearer the fringe are barely noticed, vague, or difficult to discriminate. To make the latter appear clearly, I must turn my head or cast my eyes upon them, allowing them to be situated within the central core of the visual panorama. I note that in ordinary situations it is possible to overlook or almost forget fringe phenomena altogether. Unless asked about them, I might well be unaware of them. This possibility of ignoring or forgetting fringe phenomena is important, and is a source of much error and distortion in dealing with all phenomena.

In the process initiated here, I have begun to move from first concerns with the appearance of items within the visual field, toward more general structures of the field of appearance itself. In phenomenological terms, this is the movement toward *eidetic* phenomenology or toward the concern with structures or invariants. The structures I have noted belong to the ordinary visual field; descriptively, they make sense of the flow of experience. Structures shape the possibilities of what is seen. In the visual example, the condition of the possibility for visual appearances is the shape and structure of this visual field.

What has been described above are structures within which visual appearances occur. If I generalize—which is possible only after more variations and an intensive search for counterexamples—and if the above structures hold—I can then say that these are structures of *what* is seen *as* it is seen. But precisely at this point, it is equally possible to pass over to a noetic analysis. For every point of the noematic appearance-structure of the visual panorama, a parallel set of descriptions may be made concerning the *act* of seeing. Thus, corresponding to the phenomenon that stands out in the center of the visual field, there is the act of *focusing* which I do. Moreover, this focusing can be done only within certain limits, beyond which is a fringe where focusing is no longer possible.

In most situations the thing I am actively focusing upon stands out in the core of the visual field. But there are other situations in which I respond to something in the rest of the field. If there is a bright flash off to the side, I may turn my head immediately to look for what has occurred. But in any case, whether I look for a thing actively or whether my looking follows some occurrence out there, the relation of core-focus retains a distinctive structural shape.

It turns out, then, that what is arrived at through this descriptive analysis is something more than might have been initially expected. The structure of the visual field, now considered noetically, is the structure of my visual opening to the world, that which determines and limits what and how I see. But take careful account of how this knowledge has been reached. It has not been reached directly or by accepting common belief or direct introspection. Noetically, the conclusion has been reached *reflexively*. It has been by, through, and in terms of the noematic appearances and their structures that this *existential* structure of my opening to the world has been reached.

Now, I have deliberately replaced *reflection* with *reflexivity* to emphasize the way in which ultimate self-knowledge is attained within the phenomenological procedure. I know myself only in correlation with and through the world to which I am intentionally related. This is to say, in phenomenological terms, I and world are correlated, that without world there is no I and without I there is no world (humanly conceived).

The visual world I have lightly sketched is present *for* me in a certain way and, conversely, my access to it is limited in terms of my opening to that "world." The specific shape of the correlation is the condition for my seeing things in the way they are seen. And this shape or structural feature was arrived at through a descriptive analysis of what appeared and how it appeared.

At this point some of the general features of the visual field have been noted, including two sets of noematic relations: the relation of core to field (of centered thing to its background or context) and a relation of the entire field to its fringe (horizon). If these observations are now put in their Husserlian context, it may be said that any thing seen, is seen against its background (external horizon), which etches out its distinctiveness as a figure.

With these larger features in mind, it is now possible to take a narrower look at things. I return to my examination of visual phenomena, this time casting my gaze upon a book lying upon the desk. The book appears as colored (blue), textured (cloth-like), having a certain thickness (about an inch). On its cover are a title and a name. I turn it over. Some of the previously noted characteristics remain, but now the title and name have disappeared from view, and the book presents a different *profile*.

If I pay close attention to this appearance, however, I also note that in the reversal of profiles there remains a *sense* in which the book retains its appearance as *having a backside*. In other words, in the thick, weightiness of the phenomenon-book, I continue to detect something of that which is visually absent from me. Variations can establish this sense. Note what would happen were there not this sense of absence-within-presence. First, I would be most surprised and shocked if I picked up the book and found it had no other side, that it disappeared when I turned it over. I would be surprised, but less so, if it turned out that what I thought to be the weightiness of the book was a clever disguise and that it was only a picture of a book (as in *trompe d'oeil* paintings). In short, the absence-within-presence, which is part of the sense of the phenomenon-book, is a specific kind of absence. A particular possibility belongs to the phenomenon. Even though *manifestly* presented as a profile *fulfilled* by one's looking, the book also presents a *latent* sense along with what is manifest. It has, in Husserl's language, an *inner* horizon. A complete phenomenon, then, has both a manifest profile and a latent sense. It should be noted that such an analysis is markedly different from any analysis dealing solely with the manifest presence of a phenomenon. The latter, from a phenomenological point of view, is incomplete. I do not see the world without "thickness" nor do I see it as a mere facade. What appears does so as a play of presence and a specific absence-within-presence.

I am introducing here a partial phenomenological account of perception. What is important to note in this account is the co-presence within experience of both a profile and the latently meant absence which, together, constitute the Presence of a thing. To forget or ignore the latent or meant aspect of the Presence of the thing reduces the appearance of the world to a facade, lacking weightiness and opacity. Phenomenologists also claim that what makes any object "transcendent," having genuine otherness, is locatable in this play of presence and absence-in-presence in our perceptions of things. But note that transcendence is constituted *within* experience, experience carefully analyzed.

This characterization of a thing parallels, in a limited and specific way, the previous analysis of the visual field. If I return to the visual field, now fully constituted, I am quite aware in the ordinary sense that my opening to the visual world does not exhaust that world, but is in fact a limited opening.

The seeable exceeds what I may see at any given moment or in any given gaze, and this meaning is co-present with my fulfilled seeing. Yet at the same time, whatever I do see (manifest seeing) occurs and only occurs within the limits of my opening to the world. Without the co-present significance of the genuine transcendence of the world in its presence and its absence-in-presence, the world would be a facade for me.

Thus, both the transcendence of the thing and the transcendence of the world are to be found in the sense of presence including the specific absence-in-presence that is the inner horizon of the thing on one side and the horizon of the world at the limit. The thing as a "whole" always exceeds my manifest vision, just as the world exceeds my perspective upon the world, and I sense this within and not outside experience.

I have been explaining primarily the noematic meaning of thing and world. However, a noetic correlation is also possible. The sense of transcendence tells me the limits of my opening to the world. I note that my vision is constantly, invariantly, *perspectival*. The constancy of the ratio of manifest profile to latent, but specific, sense reveals reflexively the concreteness of the *position* I occupy. What appears to me, always does so from a certain zero-ground—which I am visually. This seems an obvious discovery: I knew all along that I had a body and eyes and that I was in a certain position vis-à-vis the objects I see. But this is not my point. My point is *how* this knowledge was obtained in the present context. It was obtained reflexively, by way of the things seen, rather than directly. I discover with respect to my position that my perspectival limit, my "point of view," now becomes literally significant because of how the object appears. This retracing of a genesis of self-knowledge, of noesis through noema, is the first step in determining what Husserl called the *constitution of meaning*.

A final (though somewhat ludicrous) example points out this movement from world to I. Imagine that I attained full adulthood without knowing that I had eyes and so did not know what they were like. This notion is absurd, of course, but the absurdity stimulates thought. How *did* I discover what my eyes were like? I might have seen other people with eyes, and as I gradually discovered how like them I was, I may have concluded that I, too, had eyes. Or, I might have made the discovery through the marvel of a mirror. But what if I had no mirror; what if there were no other people with eyes? Hypothetically, I might still discover something about the structure of my eyes by purely reflexive means. From the knowledge I have attained of the shape of the visual field in terms of its noetic correlation, I might at least come to know that my visual opening to the world is roundish. So whatever my eyes might be precisely, since the boundary of my field of vision is roundish, this must be the shape of the opening through which I see. This knowledge, still incomplete, would be sheerly reflexive.

Our first excursus into phenomenological examinations has been modeled around familiar human experience. The visual field, my knowledge of my own body, the gradations and focuses of that experience, all are in some way already known. In terms of phenomenology as such, all I have introduced are certain new terms describing the structures of these experiences more precisely and illustrating the reflexive move in the constitution of self-knowledge.

What has been attained can be illustrated. Here I combine the general programmatic features of the first three chapters with the explication of the visual model of the world in this chapter:

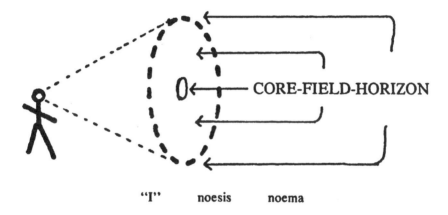

"I"   noesis   noema

In this objectification, the illustration of the correlational features of I-noesis-noema is visual. The visual field, that totality within which what is seen occurs, is the noematic field. This field is structured in terms of core-field-horizon features. Reflexively, this points back to the particular shape of the visual opening to the world, the noetic structure. Its terminus, reflexively, is the seeing "I," which is already noted to be embodied as a concrete perspective upon the world.

Although what has been developed in this chapter primarily relates to a visual model, it would be apparent that the invariants described here apply to experience in its other dimensions as well. The figure/ground relationship, for example, was noted in auditory experience as the oboe standing out from the quartet. Moreover, there are shape constants to all sensory experience, although this phenomenon has only recently been discussed in the history of thought.

If the familiarity of the visual model makes initial gains simple, this very familiarity has its own kind of resistance, complicating an adequate analysis. Up to now, I have noted what is easily seen, but now is the time to delve more deeply into that which is not so easily seen, but which lies within the richness of the visual phenomenon.

4

Illusions and Multistable Phenomena

A Phenomenological Deconstruction

In introducing the programmatic and general features of phenomenological inquiry, I have employed typical philosophers' devices. I have analyzed a totality into components and introduced a simplification. The simplification was a visual model of what is global and complex. I am quite aware that the gains in clarity may be offset by losses in richness. What is pushed to the background or, worse, forgotten, may complicate the investigation in the future. In spite of that, I shall take yet another step toward simplification by making the first area for analysis the so-called visual illusions and multistable visual phenomena.

These illusions and multistable phenomena are exceedingly familiar, and so deceptively clear. They are the sort of line drawings that appear in both philosophy and psychology textbooks, and even on placemats in restaurants. Some are two-dimensional drawings that appear to be three-dimensional, such as the Necker cube. In others, straight lines appear to be curved. All the line drawings used will be seen to have some kind of visual effect. It will be the task of a concrete phenomenological analysis to deal descriptively with these effects, illustrating in the process how phenomenological analysis goes beyond what is usually taken for granted.

I point out three things about this group of phenomena: (1) These drawings, all familiar in other texts, are simple line drawings and so, abstract. In comparison to fully etched representational line drawings by DaVinci or Michelangelo, they are bare line drawings. This clearly is part of their secret—they are from the outset suggestive in their abstractness. (2) This abstractness is a simplification of ordinary phenomena. Although these phenomena, like every visual phenomenon, display all the qualities of a plenum, they do so in a greatly simplified sense. For example, all visual phenomena show extended phenomenal color. But the multishaded phenomenon-tree with its greens, browns, blues, and other hues is a complex color plenum compared to a simple white background with black-line drawings. As Eastern sages have long known, the very blankness allows for effects not easily noted in more filled-in configurations. (3) Abstractness and simplicity are conditions for a certain ease in seeing effects, both in their familiar setting and in the more novel phenomenological setting that emerges from deconstruction. Familiarity and strangeness are here bound closely together. They give rise to perceptual games, which are simple, but not without import for the richer and more complex phenomena that can ultimately be analyzed.

I shall introduce one more simplification. In order to display a step-by-step process, often hard to detect in following actual inquiries, I shall introduce an imaginative context and assume subnormal initial perceptions. This device shows the constructive side of the deconstructions, even though normal perceivers begin at a higher level than my imaginary beginners. We are not considering what we already know; we are considering how what we know is phenomenologically constituted.

These simplifications allow the overall experimental movement of phenomenology to be seen as a movement of discovery. This movement begins with what is apparently given, but in the process of variational investigation, the initial given is progressively deconstructed and then reconstructed according to insights derived from the procedure itself. *Epoché* (the suspension of belief in accepted reality-claims) is assumed, and its function as the opening to discovery is shown. Deconstruction occurs by means of variational method, which possibilizes all phenomena in seeking their structures. In this context, *epoché* includes suspension of belief in any causes of the visual effects and positively focuses upon what is and may be seen. Equally, *epoché* excludes abstract generalizations that may apply to the drawings, but fail to account for the specific effects seen (for instance, the generalization that each example is a two-dimensional line drawing, which is true but trivial). Instead, invariants are sought that appear through the variations themselves. With this in mind, the investigation proper may begin.

In what follows I shall name each example according to one of its appearances for ease of reference in subsequent discussion. I shall employ guide pictures, smaller versions of the figures with distinctive features marked on them, in order to avoid elaborate descriptions and make the discussion easier to follow. Neither of these devices is necessary in lectures and teaching, since I can point out what is being discussed. But in the written form, if the reader is to follow the order and be clear about what occurs in each instance, different devices are required. However, the main points should be *seen* in the central, simple line drawings alone. It is important to check your own experience at each step. Of course there are some who will see what is being noted quickly, others less so.

Example One: "The Hallway"

Suppose that there is a group of observers in a room and they are presented with the following drawing:

 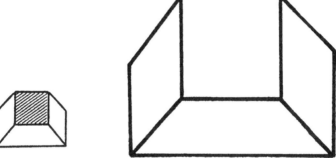

The interrogator who presents the drawing asks, "What do you see?" The response is divided. One group says that what is seen is a *hallway* (in their interpretation of the guide picture, the shaded area appears to be in the rear of the configuration as perceived three-dimensionally); the other group says that what is seen is a cut-off *pyramid* (in their interpretation of the guide picture, the shaded area appears to be forward, with the sides sloping away from it. In this case, the observer's head position approximates a helicopter pilot overhead). Ordinarily, the hallway group would see the pyramid appearance in a matter of moments, and vice-versa. But for purposes of analysis, suppose the two groups are kept apart and are stubborn in their belief about the appearance they have seen.

Within the framework of the beginning analysis, what each has seen (noema) may be paired with the, at first, literal-minded way in which the initial appearance is taken, with the following result:

Group H (hallway group) asserts: The figure *is* a hallway appearance.

Group P (pyramid group) asserts: The figure *is* a pyramid appearance.

Although differing about what "really" appears, each of these groups may be characterized as a variation upon a literal-minded impression of an initial appearance. Strictly speaking, the characterization of the way the initial appearance is taken (literal-mindedly) is a characterization of a total attitude. In this context, the specific noesis (a seeing as) occurs. At this point, both groups are at the same level:

Level I.	Noetic Context	Noema
Group H.	literal-mindedness	hallway appearance
Group P.	literal-mindedness	pyramid appearance

Both groups insist doggedly upon the validity of their reality claim with respect to appearance, but, equally, each sees something different in the configuration. Note carefully, however, that each group actually experiences the noema as claimed; they can fulfill or verify this assertion experientially, thereby offering a certain evidence for their assertion.

This situation is similar to that of the two seers of trees, the "cartesian" and the "druid"; both groups claim metaphysical certitude about what is seen. I shall call this initial certitude, *apodicticity*. To be apodictic means that I can return, again and again, to fulfill the experiential claim concerning seeing the drawing as hallway (or as pyramid).

Simplifying and reducing the example in this fashion may be burdensome to already enlightened people. Most likely, normal observers, already familiar with multistable configurations, have long since been able to see both variations alternatively. But viewers able to see either/both aspects are not at the same level of observation as our imaginary groups. They have ascended from the literal-mindedness of the first level by being able to see the alternation (of course, they see either one or the other aspect, but not both simultaneously). Their position, then, may be added as a second level of observational possibility. I shall term the group that sees either/both aspects Group A' (for ascendant).

Level I.	Noetic Context	Noema
Group H	literal-mindedness	hallway appearance
Group P	literal-mindedness	pyramid appearance
Level II.		
Group A'	polymorphic-mindedness	hallway and/or pyramid appearances

In spite of the obviousness of the polymorphic observation, several important preliminary points must be clarified even at this elementary level. First, observers of Group A' have exceeded the views of both H and P groups, at least in terms of relative comprehensiveness, since the ability to see both aspects is evidently superior to being able to see only one.

However, there is also an ascent in level. This ascent is indicated by two things that accompany ability to see alternatives. With the ascent in level, the viewer of alternatives does not lose apodicticity; he is able to return to both appearances and thus fulfill or verify the evidence of both. But the *significance* of that apodicticity changes. Once both aspects are possible, it is clear that neither the hallway nor the pyramid appearance can claim absoluteness or exhaustiveness for the possibilities of the thing.

To put this phenomenologically, the noema is now seen to contain two possibilities, and two possibilities as variations are relatively more *adequate* than one. The ascent in level is a move to (relative) *adequacy*, which now assumes a higher significance than mere apodicticity. However, it should not be forgotten that this relative adequacy is attained only through variations upon apodicticity. The fulfillability of the possibility must not be empty.

Simultaneously, the ascent in level also establishes a minimal *irreversible direction* for inquiry. This direction is nontransitive: once the ascent occurs, the observer cannot go back and recapture the naiveté of his previous literal-mindedness. While the variation upon both appearances can at any time be recaptured, the return to the claim that one, and only one, appearance is *the* appearance of the thing is now impossible. This change in the significance of apodicticity is permanent. The direction of inquiry looks thus:

Direction of Inquiry		Noetic Context	Noema	How Held
Level I.	H.	literal-mindedness	hallway	apodictic only
	P.	literal-mindedness	pyramid	apodictic only
Level II.	A'	polymorphic-mindedness	hallway/pyramid	apodictic and adequate

The direction of inquiry in which relative adequacy is more inclusive and yet retains the basic insights of the previous level can move from level I to level II, but once level II is attained, no simple reversion to level I is possible.

In the limited context of this example, in its general import, I am illustrating the first move of *epoché* and the phenomenological reductions. Husserl called for a move from the natural attitude, which is a kind of literal-mindedness imputing to things a presumed set way of being, to what he called the phenomenological attitude, here illustrated by polymorphic-mindedness. By its deliberate search for variations, the phenomenological attitude possibilizes phenomena as the first step toward getting at their genuine possibilities and the invariants inhabiting those possibilities. Potentially, the ascent to polymorphic-mindedness deliberately seeks a particular kind of *richness* within phenomena. But it also carries other implications. These may be seen if a further step-by-step discrimination of what is latent in the current example is undertaken.

Group A' has now discovered that the noema (the line drawing) contains two appearance possibilities. These are genuine apodictical possibilities of the figure. It may be said that they are *noematic* possibilities, inherent in the drawing. But all noematic possibilities are correlated with noetic acts. So far, only the context for those acts has been noted, that is, the type of beliefs surrounding the specific act that give it its implicit metaphysical background. These beliefs are *sedimented*, and the viewer may or may not be able to abandon them.

In this context of "beliefs," each viewer saw the drawing *as* something, either as a hallway or as a pyramid. (It is important to note that in all cases, the viewers saw the configuration *as* something—they did not see a bare figure and then add some significance to it.) This seeing as ——— was instantaneous. The noema appeared primitively as ———. The literal-minded viewers' first look was a naive look. They responded to what first came into view.

Such a response is typical of psychological experiments. Response times are usually limited, and the experiment is deliberately designed to eliminate reflection, critique, or extensive observation. This raises the question what such an experiment reveals, an important question in our phenomenological inquiry. It is possible that an instantaneous glance shows us something basic about perception isolated from so-called higher or lower-level conscious functions. It is equally possible that an instantaneous glance shows only what is most *sedimented* in the noetic context, the context within which perception occurs.

In both cases, the instantaneity of an initial glance must be noted with respect to the noetic act. A simple and often single noematic possibility occurs, which is correlated to the instantaneous glance. Such simplicity was noted earlier to be less than usual, since most viewers would see both alternatives within a very short time. In a psychological experiment with an increased response time, the subject sometimes reports that the figure spontaneously reversed itself. Such three-dimensional reversals are quite common, yet in the standard psychological literature, the noetic act is still noted as a relatively passive stare: If one looks at the figure long enough, "it will reverse itself."

If I had not broken down the situation into its phenomenologically ordered components, the standard accounts might seem sufficient.

Remaining within the limits of two noematic possibilities (hallway and/ or pyramid) and within the limits of two noetic contexts (literal-mindedness or polymorphic-mindedness), it is possible to go one step farther. If literal-mindedness occurs when an instantaneous glance is all that is allowed, and if initial polymorphic-mindedness is only characterized as a passive stare, what happens with a more *active* observation? This possibility is easily established by showing that the spontaneous reversal of the two appearance possibilities can occur *at will*.

The *free* variation is easily learned. Return to the hallway/pyramid figure and look at it; when one of its possibilities is fixed, blink your eyes (if necessary, name the other possibility to yourself) and aim for its alternate. Within seconds, or at most minutes, you will find that each of the variations is easily attained at will. This kind of looking is a modification of polymorphic-mindedness. It opens the way to a further stage of the inquiry.

Suppose, now, the figure is presented again, only this time there is a third response from a group of people viewing the drawing. This new group, temporarily placed at the literal-minded level, claims the figure is neither a hallway nor a pyramid, but is a *headless robot*. See this appearance or noematic possibility by returning to the drawing and the guide picture:

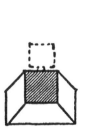 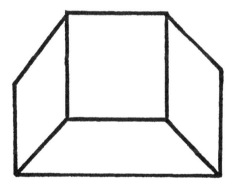

The robot has a body (the shaded area of the guide picture) and is lacking a head (the dotted outline in the guide picture). He needs to support himself with crutches (the outside vertical lines), which run from the ends of his arms (the upper diagonals) to the ground (the bottom horizontal). His legs are the lower diagonals.

Once this appearance or noematic possibility is grasped, fulfilled noetically, a rather dramatic transformation of the first two possibilities occurs. The three-dimensionality of both the hallway and the pyramid appearances is replaced by two-dimensionality; the robot is seen to be flat and standing upright. This noematic possibility is quite distinct from both the others and stands on its own, if the pun can be allowed.

How are we to integrate this possibility with the previous situation? Theoretically, it is possible to take the third group of viewers, Group R (for Robot), as an equally naive group and put them on level I, which now looks like this:

Level I.	Noetic Context	Noema
Group H	literal-mindedness	hallway
Group P	literal-mindedness	pyramid
Group R	literal-mindedness	robot

But there is something irregular about this. Empirically, the instantaneous glances allowed in the usual experiments do not produce this third group, or, if it is produced, it is a rare variation.

There seems to be a relative weight or naturalness in the first two variations, which appear three-dimensional, and not in the third, flat variation. Is it the case that in the first two variations, normal perceptual effects are being noted, while in the third something else is being shown? The question is whether an order of perception or an order of sedimentation is involved. This cannot be answered immediately, but a point can be made about the difference between the usual empirical psychology and a phenomenological psychology. Phenomenologically, the primary question concerns the structure of possibilities, the conditions for such and such empirical occurrences. Its first look is a look for possibilities and their limits, postponing any quick conclusions or generalizations from a straightforward empirical situation. Conversely, its investigation must be concrete, employing actual variations.

At the second level (polymorphic-mindedness), there also occurs a problem of integrating the robot-appearance with the previous situation. Once group A' viewers become aware of the robot appearance, they can add it to the series of variations along with the previous two variations. Group A' now has as its noematic possibilities: hallway and/or pyramid and/or robot. The direction of the inquiry—from apodicticity in each alternative to adequacy—has been maintained. (Once the third variation occurs and is established, one cannot go back to seeing the figure only as one of the three, without the changed significance of apodicticity occurring.)

This new modification of polymorphic-mindedness introduces a new variable and a new question. If what was taken to be *the* appearance of the noema has given way to two alternate appearances, and these have now given way to a third, has the range of noematic possibilities been exhausted? The discovery of a third possibility is not merely a modification of level II; rather, it introduces a new element.

The new element points to the inherent radicalism of variational method. The possibilization of a phenomenon *opens* it to its *topographical* structure. The noema is viewed in terms of an open range of possibilities and these are actively sought noetically. Thus, a special kind of viewing occurs, which looks for what is *not usually* seen. Nevertheless, what is seen is inherent in the given noema. This modification of polymorphic-mindedness is a new noetic context (open), corresponding to the possibilities of the noema (open). The significance of both noema and noesis has been modified.

Although it is possible to interpret this modification of polymorphic-mindedness as either an ascension to a new level or an intensification of the (already attained) ascendance to polymorphy, it certainly radicalizes ordinary viewing. This radicalization can be plotted on the diagram showing development of the method of inquiry as:

Level I.	Noetic Context	Noema
Group H	literal-mindedness	hallway
Group P	literal-mindedness	pyramid
Group R	literal-mindedness	robot
Level II.		
Group A'	polymorphic-mindedness	alternation hallway/pyramid (ordinary reversals)
Group A^m	polymorphic-mindedness (open possibility search)	alternation hallway/pyramid/ robot/?—(topographical possibilities)

Here, the essential features of the direction of inquiry are preserved, but have been intensified. Group A^m (ascendant modified) has more alternations than Group A' (simple ascendant as opposed to any of the literal-minded groups). *Relative* adequacy is increased and is more comprehensive than in the

ordinary alternation. Two certainties are preserved: first, all initial apodictici-
ties are retained, in that they may be experientially recaptured; second, the
direction of inquiry is certain, in that the attainment of relative adequacy is
intuitively obvious, since each new alternation makes for more adequacy than
the previous ones.

How far this procedure can go is not certain. Once alternatives are
opened, only the actual investigation can show if closure is possible.

Through the first example, I have illustrated the structure of a phenomenological inquiry, its logic of discovery. If, now, the potential attained at the
modified level of Group A^m is read back into the lower stages of observation,
one can begin to understand this procedure. The universal level of possibilization ("possibilities precede actualities in an eidetic science") includes, but
transcends, all previous levels of the possible. It preserves the validity of each
lower level in that it does not lose the ability to re-fulfill each experiential
aim. At the same time, it has ascended to a higher level of sight, which
transforms the significance of both thing and act of seeing. Suspending beliefs
(naive noetic contexts) is needed to open the possibilities of the seen to their
topographical features; otherwise, the possibilities are confined to sedimented,
ordinary viewing. The radicalized vision of modified polymorphy is not presup-
positionless, as some have claimed; it is the attainment of a new and *open*
noetic context. In Husserlian language, this attainment occurs in the switch
from the natural attitude to the phenomenological attitude.

I have used the hallway example to reveal only the first steps of the
essential shape of the phenomenological inquiry. I did not exhaust its possibilities, but though what follows might have been done in terms of this
example, I shall turn to a series of similar multistable drawings and begin a
more adequate and systematic deconstruction of their initial appearances in
order, gradually, to approximate the topography inherent in the noema and
the possibility search in a phenomenological noetic context.

5

Variations upon Deconstruction

Possibilities and Topography

With the general shape of the inquiry determined, the hermeneutic rules of procedure introduced, and one example partially analyzed, it is possible to begin variations upon a group or class of structurally similar drawings. Once again, variational method is employed to open the phenomenon to its topographical features. Such viewing looks for what is potentially there in the noema. This instantaneous glance is far from naive immediacy. It is a view seeking possibilities, as an expert investigator in a field study would look for subtle markings by which to distinguish the creatures he is observing.

For example, bird watching. The viewer notes the general configuration and silhouette of the bird and looks for minor markings, often very difficult to detect. Beginners seldom distinguish among the vast variety of sparrows, yet with visual education they soon learn to detect the different markings of song, chipping, white-throated, and other sparrows. The educated viewer does not create these markings because they are there to be discovered, but—in phenomenological language—he *constitutes* them. He recognizes and fulfills his perceptual intention and so sees the markings as meaningful. So, in what is to follow, vision is educated through a possibility search seeking the constitution of validly fulfillable variations. One aim is to arrive at a more adequate understanding of perception itself through this process.

Example Two: The Curved Line

The first drawing in this series is a very familiar one. The center lines are usually said to appear curved, whereas in reality they are straight and parallel. I call this the curved-line example:

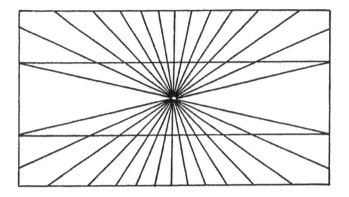

Suppose a situation similar to our previous example, that is, a group of persons observing what appears in the above drawing. Some people view this as an optical illusion, the apparent curve of the central horizontal lines being interpreted as an effect of the configuration.

However, we will begin the noetic-noematic analysis with the preliminary oversimplified situation. One group of observers sees these lines as curved; they take this to be *the* appearance of the phenomenon, and can be identified in the same way as the initially naive groups of example one.

Level I	**Noetic context**	**Noema**
Group C	literal-mindedness	curved lines

Seeing curved lines in the drawing is the normal way in which this configuration is taken in its ordinary noetic context or as sedimented in ordinary beliefs.

Furthermore, this initial appearance seems natural, so much so that a reversal does not spontaneously occur. In this example, too, certain appearance aspects seem to be privileged in normal ordinary perception. But this example is different from our first example, in that there is no reversal. Wherein, then, lies the possibility of alternate literal views or of a second level of viewing with either/both appearances?

Here, we might introduce an artifice to demonstrate that the apparently curved lines are really straight. But, given our method's demand that every variation must be actually experienceable, a problem emerges. Take the following artifice:

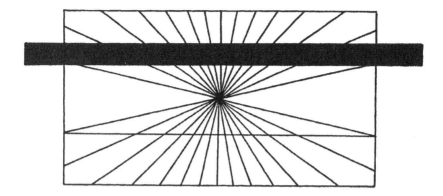

Here, an external element has been added in the form of a measuring device laid over the original drawing. Now, noting the clear parallel between the ruler and the horizontal line in the drawing, it is possible to see that the line is not curved. But this is cheating, because it radically alters the original perceptual situation. A curved-line drawing without a ruler is not the same as a curved-line drawing with a ruler. So I shall discard the artifice. If alternate possibilities are to be shown as belonging to the noema, they must be discovered *within the drawing itself*. Return to the original drawing:

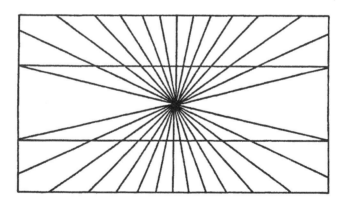

This time, look at the drawing in the following way: First, *focus* your gaze intently upon the vertex, where all the diagonal lines converge in the center of the figure. Second, deliberately see the vertex as three-dimensional and in the far distant background, that is, push the vertex back, as it were, until the diagonal lines are seen to lead to infinity. Granting that this takes a certain amount of concentration, subjects usually can do the task quickly, and then the formerly curved horizontal lines appear straight. But this is so only as long as the subject focuses upon the vertex intensely, making the horizontal lines peripheral to the central focus.

Although this kind of seeing seems artificial, we now note an alternative appearance to the drawing. Suppose that in the imaginary situation someone saw the curved-line figure first and simply as a three-dimensional distant vertex. Were that the case, we would immediately have an alternative.

Level I	Noetic Context	Noema
Group C	literal-mindedness	curved lines
Group S^f	literal-mindedness	straight lines (far apex)

Now we can compare the curved-line figure with the hallway figure, in that there is one flat appearance and one three-dimensional appearance.

In order to make the variations completely parallel to those of the hallway example, there would have to be a three-dimensional reversal possible. Return to the figure for a third time. Focus upon the vertex of the diagonal lines, but this time bring the vertex toward the very tip of your nose. That is, reverse (with effort if necessary) the direction of three-dimensionality. It may take more than one try to attain, but once you succeed note that the lines are straight when the focus is maintained upon the vertex of converging lines and the horizontal lines are peripheral.

There is a strict parallel of noematic possibilities with those of the hallway example: there are now two reversible three-dimensional appearances and one flat appearance. The direction and shape of a phenomenological inquiry occurs, with both levels, as it did in the hallway example.

Direction of Inquiry	Noetic Context	Noema
Level I		
Group C	literal-mindedness	curved lines
Group S^f	literal-mindedness	straight lines (far apex)
Group S^n	literal-mindedness	straight lines (near apex)
Level II		
Groups A^1 to A^m	polymorphic-mindedness	curved/straight^f/straight^r/?—^{n}

While the parallel of two three-dimensional and one two-dimensional possibilities is now demonstrated, there remains a curious difference between what occurred normally and what occurred with difficulty. In fact, in the curved-line example, the empirical order of discovery is the exact reverse of the hallway order. In the hallway example, the first appearances were three-dimensional and easily detected as reversible alternates; the flat, robot appearance came second and perhaps with a little initial resistance. In the curved-line example, the flat appearance with curved lines came first, while the reversible three-dimensional appearances came second and perhaps with difficulty.

Here, the question of whether an order of perception or of sedimentation of beliefs determines the empirical order becomes even more enigmatic. To assert that this inversion of empirical order is perceptual, one would have to maintain that something in the figure naturally determines the order. If one asserts that the empirical order is only the result of sedimented noetic contexts, one would have to show how this order is arbitrary. Unless something appears that distinguishes the way in which the three-dimensional effect belongs inherently to the hallway and not to the curved lines, it is possible there is a tendency to arbitrariness to the empirical order of appearances. But it is clearly too early to conclude this is definitively so.

However, at the phenomenological level of the open search for the topography of the perceptual noema, correlated with the active looking of an open possibility search, it is now the case that the two examples display the same invariant structural features, allowing at least a three-dimensional reversal and a flat appearance, regardless of the empirical order of discovery. But note that something new has been introduced into the inquiry while it is underway. I described seeing the first example as (like) ——— in terms of a kind of story. The drawing appeared as (like) a hallway, or as (like) a pyramid, or as (like) a headless robot. Once the appearance had been named, the observer could easily identify the noematic possibility. This story device, a metaphorical naming, connects the abstract figure with something familiar. The context of familiarity is such that the names are names of ordinary well-known things.

Suppose, when considering the hallway example, we found empirically that all the members of the hallway group were carpenters. They were accustomed to building hallways—in fact, that is almost all they ever did. In this case, the order of appearance would not be surprising at all. Plainly, carpenters who build hallways are likely to see the abstract drawing as something familiar. If we discovered that all those who saw the figure as a cut-off pyramid were pyramid builders, there would be no surprise about the order. At level one, the same goes for the robot group.

Of course, the story device is not neutral. It allows or suggests a certain way for the perceptual act to take shape. But it does so indirectly. One does not have to know what one is doing perceptually to have the appearance coalesce as a hallway or a pyramid or even a robot, once the appearance is recognized as such. One sees spontaneously, once the suggestion is made. This is not to say that the appearances could not have been discovered without names; a story device simply provides an easy and unself-conscious way for the appearances to be noted.

However, while a story device could have been used in the curved-line example, it would have been secondary. For the new element was a set of direct instructions about how to look: focus upon the vertex and then push the lines either forward or back, either toward infinity or to your nose. (As a passing observation, those who are highly successful in pushing the lines to infinity and back again can learn to do this on a continuum, so that the horizontal lines may be seen to be straight, gradually curve, and then re-straighten.) Here, a direct connection can be made with a feature of both the visual field and the noetic act: a ratio between what is focal and what is fringe.

The direct instructions given to the viewer of the curved-line figure deliberately modify the normal or ordinary way the figure is initially taken. In a short glance resulting in the flat variation, the figure is taken as a whole, a totality. The entire figure appears within a wide focus. But under the instructions on how to see, that focus is modified to a narrow focus, with the results already noted.

Phenomenologically interpreted, this is to say that the way in which noetic shape (focusing) is modified is a condition for the possibility of seeing certain shapes rather than other noematic appearances. Nor was this feature absent from the hallway example, though there the role of focus was indirect. In the hallway example, I drew attention by the device of the guide picture, to a particular aspect of it: the central square. In both the hallway and the pyramid possibilities, this indirect focal act played its part. But when the headless robot figure occurred, there was a deliberate, although indirect, drawing of focus away from the central square. Mentioning the absent head, the arms and legs, and the ground on which the robot stood, provided a wide focus and so a flat configuration to the figure. The noetic act functioned to allow this different possibility to emerge.

Here, we move toward resolving the question of whether perceptual or sedimented order controls the way in which empirical orderings occur, but the advance transforms the question. On the one hand, the empirical order clearly contains habitual sediments affecting how a particular configuration is taken. Yet on the other hand, in all appearances, a certain structural feature of perception is operative (in this case, focus—with the added possibility of three-dimensional effect).

For the moment, note two different strategies of interpretation within the investigation. The use of story devices and (metaphorical) naming I shall call a *hermeneutic* strategy. In a hermeneutic strategy, stories and names are used to create an immediate noetic context; they derive their power of suggestion from familiarity or from elements of ordinary experience. The story creates a condition that immediately sediments the perceptual possibility. In untheoretical contexts, this has long been used to let someone see something. Storytellers, mythmakers, novelists, artists, and poets have all used similar means to let something be seen. Plato, at the rise of classical philosophy, often paired a myth or fable with argument or dialectic. Within the context set by the story, experience takes shape.

But, note what happens in terms of the functions and structures of perception in the hermeneutic strategy: neither has to be known (theoretically) nor do directions about how to see occur. Instead, there is a gestalt-event. All at once, the desired effect is achieved; one sees it in an instant. And even if the shift from what was expected or ordinarily taken is dramatic and radically different, once it occurs it is so obvious that one wonders why it was not seen in that way before.

Ultimately, the hermeneutic strategy places its primary emphasis upon language. The symptomatic use of language as a story device illustrates the point. Perception takes shape within and from the power of suggestion of a language-game. It sees according to language. This strategy is the basis of what has become known as *hermeneutic phenomenology*. Historically, the preeminent figure working it out was Martin Heidegger, but Paul Ricoeur also took this direction.

Hermeneutic strategy tends to place its emphasis upon a noematic weighting, although in a somewhat unusual sense. The story lets something be seen; thus, what stands out is the noematic possibility. *How* this occurs, at least in terms of the mechanisms of perception, is less important than *that* it occurs or can occur in the ways open from the topography of the noema. In terms of another long tradition of philosophy, a hermeneutic strategy is more likely to be realist, insofar as it gives a certain precedence to the thereness of the noema. Language is the means, the primary relation, of the condition for the possibility of this discovery.

The second strategy I shall call a *transcendental* strategy. By this I mean that, like transcendental philosophy with its theme centering upon the subject, the way in which perception functions is made thematic. This is the counterpart to the hermeneutic strategy and can be seen to function with a certain *noetic* tendency.

The instructions on how to look rely on a certain knowledge of the mechanisms of perception and on a turn to the subject as active perceiver. This noetic turn stresses the activity of viewing as the condition for the possibility of the object appearing as it does. In its most extreme form, particularly in the work of Edmund Husserl, its tendency is to emphasize the constitution of meaning done by the subject. In terms of the usual traditions of philosophy, this gives the transcendental strategy an idealist emphasis.

Transcendental strategy, however, is also analytic in its procedure. If one knows enough about the structures of perception, ideally, one should be able to deduce, or at least predict, which effects will eventually occur. One may guide viewing from the knowledge of its structural possibilities.

Yet both of these strategies, in spite of a tendency to emphasize one or the other of the correlational foci, point up the same phenomena and utilize variational method to achieve the ultimate understanding of invariance, limits and range of possibilities. In continuing the analysis of multistable examples, I shall utilize both strategies and attempt to demonstrate how a knowledge of invariants is built up in the process.

6

Expanded Variations and
Phenomenological Reconstruction

The analysis of bimorphic examples in the two previous chapters proved inadequate in their simplicity. The following analysis undertakes a further probing into the topography of similar drawings, with an eye to attaining greater and greater degrees of adequacy.

Example Three: The Cube Series

The following three instances of multistable phenomena consist of variations upon the well-known Necker cube. In the standard psychologies, this figure is usually said to reverse itself spontaneously in two three-dimensional appearances. If the cube is viewed (in ordinary, passive gazing) over a period of time, its three-dimensionality reverses itself.

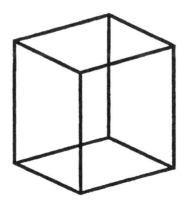

In accordance with the already established phenomenological analysis, this reversal can be noted as two variations of polymorphy. (Since the examples in this chapter are polymorphic, the literal-minded characteristics of level one do not apply; for this reason, level one can be dispensed with for the remainder of this inquiry.) These two appearances are three-dimensional reversals of a cube. In this respect, the cube example displays an empirical order contiguous with the hallway example: at the polymorphic level, the noetic-noematic analysis shows one noematic possibility with a forward three-dimensional aspect, the other with a rearward aspect. In the diagram below, $Cube^f$ symbolizes the forward aspect, $Cube^r$, the rearward.

Level II	**Noesis**	**Noema**
Polymorphy (A^m)	seeing as $\longrightarrow$	$Cube^f/Cube^r/$? . . . n

Here, the slight change in the diagram assumes that the polymorphic level has been established, and interest lies solely in the multiple possibilities. I also assume the observations to be active ones situated within the open noetic context of phenomenological inquiry. Empirically, the first appearances are two and have been arranged in the either/both alternative order.

Two further points concerning this stage of inquiry should be noted. First, the symbol, ? . . . n, as used in the diagram, suggests an open search for greater and greater relative adequacy. An active search must be made for further possibilities: What noematic possibilities can the figure contain? Only after an adequate, or at least sufficient, number have been discovered can further claims be made about invariances and the topography of the phenomena. Here we have a problem—we do not know how far such possibilities extend—and a question—how do these possibilities arise?

Second, now that the noematic possibilities have been narrowed down to topographical possibilities (as yet open), the noesis must be similarly narrowed down. In the changed diagram the wider framework of the noetic context is presupposed, but now the specific structure of the noetic stance must also be clarified. Phenomenologically, this is done in correlation with the noematic possibility where the noesis is reflexively noted.

If I return to the figure and its reversal, I can note something about the transition. In the process of reversal, the figure seems to move. Giving way from its first stabilization to its second stabilization, it jumps, apparently in motion, before being fixed again. If there is a change in noematic aspect, can a correlation be noted noetically? According to the previous analysis, with respect to visual noema, there was a reflexive reference to the perspectival position of the viewer. Here, the clue for noetic change is discovered.

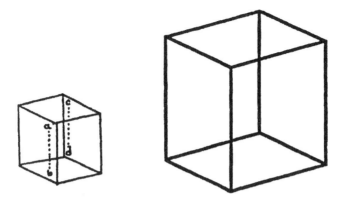

(The guide picture is inserted in order to identify key features.)

If I return to the reversal transition and query the perspectival position in the two appearances of the cube, I find that there is indeed a corresponding change. This can be put as a conditional (as if). In the guide picture, the most forward vertical line in its forward reversal appears to be line a-b. Noetically, the position of the viewer is as if he were somewhat above the figure, looking down at it. In the reversal, this noetic position shifts isomorphically with the shift in noematic appearance. In the rearward reversal, the most forward line is c-d, and the position of the viewer is as if the cube were being seen from below, the viewer looking up at it. This shift in noetic positions can be detected in the transition from one noematic possibility to the other. The isomorphism of noema-noesis in both its noematic appearance and the noetic position can be diagrammed correlatively:

Level II	Noesis	Noema
	seeing as (P^d)	Cube^f
Polymorphy	seeing as (P^u)	Cube^r
	? . . . . . n	? . . . . . n

Here "p" stands for noetic position and "u" and "d" symbolize the upward or downward perspectives. Note that the downward perspective correlates with the forward and the upward with the rearward cube appearances: *I* look downward, or *I* look upward from my position.

Once this factor is noted reflexively, it is possible to refine the awareness of position as a guide to increasing *control* over the noematic appearances. For instance, to make the cube reverse itself rather than allow it spontaneously to reverse itself, I first see it in whichever three-dimensional appearance it shows itself, then I blink (perhaps saying to myself the name of its reversed appearance), and with a little practice, I soon get the variant I want. I can refine this practice by "placing myself" in position to see either the downward or upward and thus get the variant required. Furthermore, in this shift of position, I also change the central point of focus for the two variants. For the downward position of looking at the forward facing cube, I focus concentratedly at the point "a," whereas in the reversal, I shift the focus to point "c."

This development is clearly a kind of noetic training relying upon basically transcendental strategy, which takes the shape of instructions on how to see. However, it is important to remain within the topographical limits of the phenomenon. The variations must be variations of the phenomenon and not visualized imaginative additions. They must be perceptual variants of the cube.

Noetically, three structural possibilities have been isolated: (1) the *ratio* of focus to fringe, which is controllable within the limits of vision, (2) the point of focus from which the field expands and shifts, and (3) a shift in relative position with respect to the noema. In each case there remains an isomorphism, a strict correlation, between noema and noesis. Only, strategically, the emphasis has been placed momentarily on the noetic side. However, this device accumulates clues that expand the search for significant variations within the topography of the multistable phenomenon.

Return again to the cube. At this point, two alternations have been noted; these appear in empirical order and have the same effect as the hallway example. If the cube displays the same topographical possibilities as the hallway, a flat appearance should also be found. But the sedimented recalcitrance of the natural attitude is complicated in this instance by two factors: the cube drawing is more complex and has more elements than the hallway; this complexity precludes easy and immediate identification with any ordinary object. This is not to say that a flat appearance is impossible to attain, only that, empirically, the degree of recalcitrance in attaining flat variations is higher than that for the hallway figure (although its order remains the same).

If the noetic transcendental strategy is followed, there is one tactic for allowing the flat configuration to occur that should work. In the hallway and the curved-line examples, the flat or two-dimensional gestalt occurred with a widened unconcentrated focus. It should thus be possible to widen one's focus deliberately, avoiding concentration on any point in the figure, and attain a flat or two-dimensional appearance. With some effort, this succeeds, though stability is more difficult to maintain than with the two previous variations.

However, it is always more difficult to attain gestalts with the transcendental strategy of instructions on how to view than with the noematically oriented hermeneutic strategy. If a background story can be found to allow the third variation to appear, its stability will coalesce almost instantaneously. Suppose, now, that the cube drawing is not a cube at all, but is an insect in a hexagonal opening:

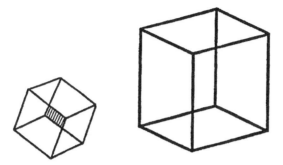

This view can be accomplished if the central parallelogram (shaded area in the guide picture) is seen as the insect's body, its six legs being the lines stretching to the sides of the hexagon (which may be a hole or whatever). Once again, the noematic gestalt emerges simply through the device of a story. The imaginative background leads perception into this possibility.

The cube example now shows the same topographical possibilities as the hallway and curved-line examples. Thus, an initial weak generalization can be made about the topographical features of all three drawings. The parallelism is indicated below, with the dimensional aspects symbolized as indicated, where $3\text{-}d^f$ means three-dimensional forward; $3\text{-}d^r$, rearward and $2\text{-}d$, two-dimensional. The numbers in parentheses indicate the empirical order of seeing; (1) is first in empirical order of seeing, (2) is second.

Topographical Possibilities

Hallway	$3\text{-}d^f$ (1)/ $3\text{-}d^r$ (1)/ $2\text{-}d$ (2)
Cube	$3\text{-}d^f$ (1)/ $3\text{-}d^r$ (1)/ $2\text{-}d$ (2)
Curved line	$3\text{-}d^f$ (2)/ $3\text{-}d^r$ (2)/ $2\text{-}d$ (1)

In terms of apriori possibilities, each figure shows the same topography, but in terms of empirical order with degrees of recalcitrance to deconstruction to pure topographical possibilities, the curved-line example's order is inverse to that of the hallway and cube (symbolized by the numbers in parentheses).

The demonstration establishing the same topographical possibilities is still not complete. Furthermore, the enigma of whether the recalcitrance of the empirical order of possibilities is due to sedimentation of habitual beliefs or to perceptual factors remains unresolved. Resolution calls for a still more radical phenomenological procedure.

The polymorphy discovered in the three examples is not adequate for a full descriptive analysis of topographical possibilities. Once more I return to the cube with a more radical intent and a more active search for topographical possibilities. These must be intentionally fulfillable to count as evidence in the accumulation of depth structures of multistable phenomena. I revert to the hermeneutic strategy:

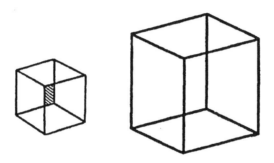

Suppose I tell you that the cube is not a cube at all, but is a very oddly cut gem. The central facet (the shaded area of the guide picture) is nearest you, and all the other facets are sloping downward and away from it. Once this is seen (it may take a moment or two for the gestalt to occur), note what happens. First, a completely new three-dimensional appearance results, one not at all in keeping with the original three-dimensional appearance of the cube. Second, the significance of the various elements and lines in the drawing are rearranged with the new gestalt. The story has allowed a new configuration to be seen.

Now, suppose I tell you that the gem is also reversible and give a new story to let this be seen. Suppose you are now inside the gem, looking upward, so that the central facet (the shaded area of the guide picture) is the one farthest away from you, and the oddly cut side facets are sloping down toward you. When this appearance occurs, there exists a fifth possibility for the cube example. Prior to further interpretation, the gain in topographical insight may be shown:

Topographical Possibilities

Cube $3\text{-}d^f$ $/3\text{-}d^r$ $/2\text{-}d$ $/3\text{-}d^{f''}$ $/3\text{-}d^{r''}$ $/? \ldots . \text{ n}$
      (cube fore)   (cube rear)   (flat)   (gem fore)   (gem rear)

The polymorphy of the cube example is now more open than ever. Five possibilities have been discovered as genuine topographical possibilities of the drawing. The hermeneutic strategy has allowed noematic possibilities to be seen. Imaginary contexts permit easy gestalts to occur. Here, a careful distinction should be made. The imaginary context is a background context. It does not add anything visual to the noematic possibility of the drawing in the sense of visually projecting something on the configuration. When such a visualistic, imaginary projection is done, it is clearly of quite a different order from continuing to treat the drawing as an open geometric configuration.

If a visual and imaginary projection added color to the gem, it would be possible to *imagine* it as red or blue by adding that visual imaginary component. But that is not what the background context does. Rather, background context offers a shortcut to noematic gestalts by providing for a spatial arrangement to occur.

Once the fourth and fifth noematic possibilities have been exhibited, it is possible to parallel the hermeneutic device with its transcendental counterpart, which emphasizes the noetic correlate. Noting, for the moment, only those structural features of perceptual change that occur noetically, it can be seen that there are subtle changes in focus between the cube as cube, and the cube as a gem. The core aspect of the gem appearance is the central facet. In the cube appearance, either point "a" or point "c" is central, or focus depends on positionality: the downward or upward. It is evident that a noetically controlled search parallels the imaginary, hermeneutic search. Instead of telling a story that allows the gestalt to appear, it might be possible to continue changing focal points, to scan and gaze at new configurations much more analytically than through hermeneutic devices. This process removes the latent suspicion that a hermeneutic device adds something to the figure, and it appeals to the abstract and geometric-minded. But such a noetic device is slower and harder to describe initially, and it has to be cast in a tight technical language presupposing substantial understanding of perceptual structures.

This variation upon the two phenomenological strategies indirectly points the way in which most of these discoveries have occurred. It has been observed that creative discoveries are often first cast in metaphorical terms and that soft logics precede hard logics. Here, a repeated generation of initial noematic discovery through hermeneutic devices with later reflexive gains in the transcendental mode, is significant.

Regardless of which strategy is used in the expansion of polymorphy through a more radical phenomenological investigation, the direction of inquiry remains open with respect to adequacy. In moving step by step, it is advisable to consolidate gains, particularly as long as the empirical order is felt to conflict with the apriori order of topographical possibilities.

In the standard psychologies, a variation of the Necker cube is frequently used as the second example of a cube appearance:

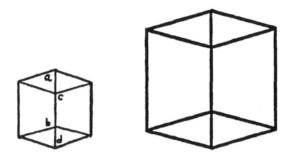

Without much effort, particularly in the light of what is beginning to be a re-sedimentation of noetic context, it is possible to duplicate the initial variations simply:

Variation 1:   The new cube is seen to be facing forward with its three-dimensional effect seen from above, paralleling the former cube appearance, 3-d^f. (Line a-b is forward as in the guide picture.)

Variation 2:   A reversal of the above (line c-d in guide picture forward), 3-d^r.

Variation 3:   A two-dimensional appearance, which is usually somewhat easier to see with this drawing than with the previous one.

Although three variations upon the drawing is one more than most standard psychologies admit, phenomenologically it should be suspected that at least two more variations are possible, as with the first cube drawing.

Briefly resorting to the story device, it is relatively simple to establish variations four and five. In variation four, suppose you are lying flat on your back, looking upward at the underside of a small, medieval church ceiling. The ridge of the ceiling (line c-b in the guide picture) is farthest from you, the sides slope down toward you as if to meet upright walls. This is variation 3-d$^{r''}$. A reversal of this new and quite different three-dimensional appearance is possible. Suppose you are now above the church, looking down on the roof. The ridge of the roof (line c-b) is central and nearest your position, the sides now slope downward, away from your position. This establishes variation 3-d$^{r'''}$.

The five variations noted for the first cube drawing are now established for the second cube drawing:

Topographical Possibilities

Cube^2 3-d$^{f'}$ /3-d$^{r'}$ /2-d/3-d$^{f''}$/3-d$^{r''}$/? . . . n

If my step-by-step examples have been followed carefully, it should be getting easier to see alternatives. Phenomenologically interpreted, this education of vision suggests that the usual recalcitrance of a sedimented noetic context is loosening.

Experiencing a certain loosening of ordinary expectations, the viewer begins to suspect that all abstract drawings (insofar as they belong to this type) are more polymorphic than they are usually taken to be. Noematically, polymorphy is far more open to multiple stabilities than the naive first glance, which gives only one or two, or even three possible stabilities. This new ease of deconstruction may be shown by a rapid demonstration of a third cube drawing which also is frequently seen in standard psychologies.

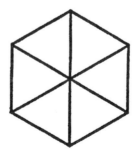

In the above figure, an initial empirical order different from the other cube drawings is likely. Its flat, two-dimensional appearance (i.e., as a hexagon) is likely to be seen first. In fact, the naive viewer might not even suspect it to

be a cube if it were not deliberately placed in a series of cube drawings. Here again, sedimentation shows itself as the noetic context of the possibilities of appearance. What first appears does so in terms of familiarity and expectation within ordinary experience.

In order to vary empirical order, suppose the flat appearance occurs first. I shall elicit variations 3-d$^{f'''}$ and 3-d$^{r'''}$ prior to the cube appearances. The first non-cube three-dimensional appearance will occur if you suppose you are lying on your back, looking upward, inside a teepee. The intersection of the lines is the top where the teepee poles cross, and the sides are slanting down toward you on the ground. The reversal occurs when you suppose you are above the teepee, as if in a helicopter, looking down at it. Now the sides are slanted downward from the intersection.

The empirical order in this case has developed as 2-d/3-d$^{r''}$/3-d$^{f''}$, which is quite different from that established in the other examples. It is obvious by now that this example has no natural order. Indeed, once these three variations on cube^3 have been constituted, it is momentarily difficult to see cube^3 as a cube (the first empirical appearances for cube^1 and cube^2). But minor recalcitrance is not the same as impossibility. To constitute variations 3-d$^{f'}$ and 3-d$^{r'}$ you must intend a cube. To obtain the 3-d appearance in the forward-facing variation, focus on line a-b, as nearest you. This constitutes 3-d^f with an upward angle. To obtain the reverse, shift your apparent position and look downward, the line c-d marking the near angle facing you.

The order in which the five variations on cube^3 occurred is:

Topographical Possibilities

Cube^3 2-d/3-d$^{r''}$/3-d$^{f''}$/3-d$^{f'}$/3-d$^{r'}$ / ? . . . n

Clearly, however, this order was not a necessity and it could have been established differently.

Unless the hexagonal-type drawing is introduced in the cube series as below, its cube appearances are not intuitively obvious to naive experience.

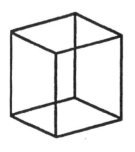 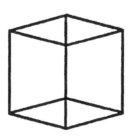 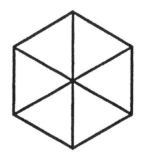

The series itself sets an initial context. Taking them initially as variations upon a cube, it is possible to go through the three-dimensional reversals in each of the drawings quickly. But it is increasingly likely that the empirical order is set by the sedimentation of an initial context.

We gain advantages from this conclusion: the role of context and sedimentation is increasingly isolated and its functions are observed. The phenomenological deconstruction, which throws doubt upon the primacy of empirical order, achieves two results. The role of context and sedimentation emerges as a possible theme for investigation; the gradual constitution of topographical possibilities frees the noema to assume its full richness and complexity.

Once these two regions (often confused in standard psychologies) are freed, it is possible to thematize each separately. Thematization is a reconstruction along phenomenological lines, in each case driving toward the structure of possibilities. On the side of the topography of the noema, subsequent phenomenological analysis deals with the range, structure, and horizons of possible variations within the open context of phenomenological viewing. Here, the aim is to isolate and describe the structural properties of the class of multistable phenomena. On the other side, not yet as thoroughly thematized, it is possible to envision a set of investigations into sedimented contexts as a related region of inquiry.

While the topography of the multistable phenomenon and the structure and function of the immediate context have not been exhausted, phenomenological deconstruction and the opening to a reconstruction within the limits of the phenomenon are significant steps beyond the initial situation with which the inquiry began. The objects of the inquiry—multistable phenomena—should appear in different ways to the now educated vision.

Compare the initial situation of vision with its current state, presuming that the exercises have been followed and fulfilled as indicated in each step. If the phenomenological education of vision has occurred, as it should, the following may be considered as relevant conclusions:

I. Initially, the phenomena (the drawings I have shown) appeared in one or two variations. This is always the case with most naive viewers, but interestingly, it is also the case with most standard psychologies.[1] In the psychologies, multistability is usually interpreted to be a bimorphic phenomenon and it is assumed that this is all the phenomenon contains. If a third variation is pointed out, it is usually regarded as odd or weaker in stability than the normal bimorphic reversal.

Contrastingly, within the purview of the phenomenological deconstruction with its concentration upon topographic possibilities, it is now seen that at least five possibilities may be obtained, and that once cleared from their initial sedimentations, these variations can be stabilized, easily attained, and repeated.

This opening of the possible significance of the phenomenon is the result of *epoché* and the phenomenological reductions, which deliberately put aside ordinary assumptions and sediments—do violence to them, as it were—in order to free the phenomenon for its essential, rather than accidental, appearances. In ordinary and even standard psychological viewing, topographical possibilities do not show themselves spontaneously apart from the immediate and larger background noetic contexts. *Epoché* displaces that natural attitude or already sedimented context from the outset.

In ordinary and standard psychological views, a topographical possibility either does not show itself at all (I am not aware of any development of topography in the literature of psychology along the lines developed here), or it is discovered accidentally and usually dismissed.[2] Yet the implications of polymorphy are extremely important for both empirical and epistemological studies.

II. Once the phenomenon has been opened to a topographical investigation and its potential wealth discovered, a series of second-order gains may be discerned as well. The *eidetic* level is reached, and deeper layers of the invariants may be seen in the phenomenon. For example, it is evident, that all multistable drawings of the type being investigated should display more than one or two variants, and that something structural in polymorphy allows this multiplicity.

This leads to a second-order deconstruction of presuppositions about perception and the sedimented context. For example, the farther the investigator goes with the examination of multistable phenomena, the more likely it is that he will discover ever more quickly and easily a whole range of topographical possibilities in subsequent drawings. At the least, this shift from ordinary to open noetic contexts ruins the phenomenological investigator as a naive subject. For every group of phenomena being interrogated, ascendance to the open context is irreversible. In addition, it becomes more and more apparent that the empirical order depends on the way ordinary or commonsense contexts are sedimented, rather than on perceptual structure, as such. In fact, once expectation of polymorphy is thoroughly consolidated, any variation in a multistable drawing can occur first.

This is not yet apparent in most standard psychological theories. People whose viewpoint is based on ordinary experience and certain theoretical commitments are reluctant to give up long-held expectations and assumptions. In discussing this material with psychologists, I have learned to predict a progressive reticence about the tenacity of sedimented theoretical views. It is usually a relatively simple matter to show that the phenomenon displays the perceptual possibilities demonstrated; once experientially verified, the phenomenon cannot be denied (apodicticity). But the implication of polymorphy is not often so quickly grasped. In the progressive reluctance to put aside assumptions, it is usually held that only the first one, two, or at most, three variations belong naturally to the phenomenon. All others are odd, or the constructions of an overactive imagination.

Yet neither of these viewpoints can hold. With practice, the odd ones become less odd, and each variation attains full stability and naturalness in a very short time. The order of appearance-variations becomes increasingly arbitrary. Experiential intuition itself is changing; as it does so, the sense of what is natural and of what is given also changes. Of course, in an empirical study using naive subjects (viewers who are not phenomenologically trained) with the usual experimental controls, only one or two variations will be noted. But this is to be expected, precisely because the ordinary viewer holds to a certain noetic context. Indeed, this background context is itself gradually being explicated in the process of this investigation.

Furthermore, the significance of the empirical study must be reinterpreted from the phenomenological point of view. If an instant glance, coupled with a strongly held but naive, ordinary noetic context, responds to the expected first appearance only, it is evidence of current sediment shape, rather than evidence of a primary characteristic of perception. While not denying the importance of empirical studies, phenomenologists must consider unacceptable those claims whose premise is limited by the present definition of empirical evidence. Phenomenologically, the structures of perception are more likely to be discovered through variational method, which investigates the whole range of possibilities from those of ordinary sediments to the most extreme horizontal possibilities.

Additionally, holding that odd cases are imaginative constructions does not protect the standard psychologies or ordinary experience from the potential loosening of long-held assumptions in the phenomenological experiment. Such imaginary backgrounds always relate to what is seen. To call the configurations in the cube series "cubes" is already to have named them. A named geometrical figure is as much an imaginary concept as the named insect figure that allowed the two-dimensionality of the cube to appear. Perception does not occur apart from language, and it is just as possible for names to lead experience as it is for experience to arrive at names. And if one follows the longer, indirect route of transcendental strategy, which instructs one how (and not what) to see, one arrives at the same effects, albeit tediously and painfully, without any hint of imaginary construction. The possibilities of polymorphy are the topographical possibilities of the thing itself as an open noema.

III. At this point in our discussion of *how* we see *what* we see, a substantial sense of change in our perception of the way things may be seen should have occurred. The ordinary viewer allows things to be seen in the sedimented context of ordinary beliefs. Because we are culturally familiar, not only with cubes, but also with drawings of cubes, the cube example appears first as a cube. The standard psychologies themselves are part of the belief-furniture of our ordinary universe.

Phenomenological observations do violence to the passivity of ordinary viewing. There is a deliberate probing of the phenomenon for something that does not at first show itself, and a growing sense of control over what is seen. This control has two aspects: one, it is able to elicit from the phenomenon what was not at first seen, and two, it obtains exactly the variations demanded in the order demanded. In the process, a new type of familiarity is constructed, the familiarity of polymorphy. There is a playfulness here akin to the playfulness found in artistic contexts. However, the free variations of the artist are given systematic and scientific purpose in the investigation of essential features and limits of a given phenomenal region.

In each of these three conclusions, we may speak of an ascent to the phenomenological attitude. If consolidated, this ascent is no longer a theoretical device, but becomes a permanent part of our conceptual machinery. Late in his career, Husserl noted precisely this: "It is to be noted also that the present, the 'transcendental' *epoché* is meant, of course, as a habitual attitude which we resolve to take up once and for all. Thus it is by no means a temporary act which remains incidental and isolated in its various repetitions."[3]

7

Horizons

Adequacy and Invariance

The phenomenological ascent, it should be evident, transforms both the sense of what is given and the understanding of how experience occurs. In ordinary experience a certain inflexibility is assumed to belong to givenness; a hallway and a cube appear naturally and obviously as what they are empirically taken to be. This is considered a *fact*-stratum concerning things and constitutes the naive sense of givenness. After phenomenological deconstruction, givenness is loosened so that the empirical order shows itself to be a result of an unstated context of beliefs. This movement from naivete to openness, increases with ever expanded adequacy over what is merely apodictic. Topographical possibilities replace the initial *fact*-stratum with an *essence*-stratum. All occurrences that exemplify facts take their place as variations upon an essential insight.

This is not to say that all givenness disappears, but that the significance of the given is transformed. Givenness in its phenomenological context becomes what is fulfillable. This is what is meant in Husserlian language by an experiential intuition. Any intentional aim that can be fulfilled is intuitively evident. (This language comes from Husserl's mathematical background; he carried it over into phenomenology.) The fulfillability of facts remains possible at both the given and the intentional level, with the changed significance noted. Thus, the experiments we have been conducting can be called intuitional demonstrations. The type of intuition involved is similar to logical or mathematical intuition in terms of what is usually called self-evidence. Once a variation is seen, there can be no doubt that it has been seen, and its strength is like that of logical insight, but this time, in the region of perceptual experience. It is in this sense that phenomenology claims to be an essential or apriori science.

The fulfillability of the series of intuitional demonstrations is what remains as the core sense of givenness after the phenomenological deconstruction of what is first taken to be the case in ordinary experience. At the same time, this direction of ascent, which becomes operational for continued variations, drives toward an adequate understanding of the phenomena. However, the phenomenological level of operation is faced with a problem quite different from that of the empirical level, in that openness rather than facticity becomes problematic. The problem with open adequacy can be illustrated by following one more multistable example through a series of variations. I shall call this the circle example.

The Circle Example

The expectation that this figure will yield a series of variations is now part of a phenomenologically sedimented noetic context. But until the variations are performed and made intuitively evident, it is unclear how many and of what type they may be. Since empirical order has been largely replaced by an apriori order, it may be interesting to generate variations arbitrarily, making a parallel with the cube examples.

In the previous examples, the order appeared as first three-dimensional (easy), and then two-dimensional (initially more difficult), variations, symbolized as 3-d^f/3-d^r/2-d. . . . Suppose these variations are to be displayed by the circle example. Initially, utilizing the hermeneutic strategy, the 3-d^f appearance can be seen as a giant clam standing on edge. The circle is a clam. The squiggled line is its mouth, which is curved and facing the viewer. The sides of the shell curve around from the mouth. This gives a three-dimensional forward-facing variation.

Once three-dimensionality is seen, its reversal is possible. Suppose you are inside the clam, looking at its mouth from the inside. The mouth makes a convex curve, farthest from you at the center and nearest where it meets the circumference of the circle; thus, 3-d^r. Two-dimensionality is simple in this drawing, since the figure might as well be a circle with a squiggled line through it. If you like, it is a wire mobile hanging from the ceiling with a squiggled wire running through the middle. Here the order parallels that seen in the cube examples: 3-d^f/3-d^r/2-d/ / . . . n.

Other variations are possible for an arbitrary order, for example, variation four is similar to the Janus-faced appearances of duck-rabbits and the Peter-Paul Goblet in which a figure/ground reversal occurs. For this variation, see the circle as a bimorphic cameo. The lefthand side of the circle is the face of the cameo, while the righthand side is the background. I shall symbolize this variation as 2-d^{dr} (dr for dominant right). Variation five is the reversal, the righthand side being the face and the lefthand side being the background. This may be symbolized as 2-d^{dl} (dl for dominant left). At this point there are now five variations, three of which are two-dimensional variations:

Topographical Possibilities

Circle   3-d^f/3-d^r/2-d/2-d^{dr}/2-d^{dl}/? . . . n

There are now five variations, though without a strict parallel with the cube, since there are two three-dimensional and three two-dimensional variations. The two-dimensional variations, however, suggest that several noetic possibilities are active. Shift, then, to a noetic emphasis for a moment, and take note of these. The circle figure is clearly open to plays upon dominance and recessiveness, such as are already well known as figure/ground reversals in Gestalt psychology. Supposing a purely topographical projection, it should be possible to combine two noetic possibilities—figure/ground possibilities and three-dimensional possibilities—to constitute even more perceptual variants.

To make this point simply, I revert to the hermeneutic strategy (stories). I shall also temporarily employ guide pictures and the device of turning the figure on its axis. But neither of these external devices are necessary, except for convenience, simplicity, and directness.

In the next variations, dominance, recessiveness and three-dimensional effects are combined. Suppose you are looking through the periscope of a submarine. On the horizon (in the ordinary, not phenomenological, sense), the ocean (the shaded area in the lefthand guide picture) is dominant, with the sky above, recessive and open. Here, the circle is the hole close to your eyes, through which you peer, while the ocean is more distant and the sky more distant yet. I shall symbolize this sixth variant as 3-$d^{d-r'}$ (d-r' for dominance-recessive prime).

An inversion of variation six is possible. Suppose you are looking into a cave through its opening. The dominant upper half of the circle (righthand guide picture) is the foreground, and consists of stalactites hanging from the roof of the cave; the bottom, recessive half is the floor of the cave, which continues into the distance. Variation seven may be symbolized as 3-$d^{r-d'}$ (recessive and dominance reversed).

Nor do seven variations exhaust the intuitable possibilities of the circle example. When this example is used in classrooms at this juncture in teaching variational method, ten to fourteen variations are discovered by the students who have grasped the principle of topographical possibilities. Most of these, of course, are further variations upon the elements already noted.

Such variations may be predicted and fulfilled easily if the insight into the topographically essential traits of multistable figures has been grasped. For instance, variations upon three-dimensionality are made by projecting from the known elements toward those not yet known, and fulfillments attempted accordingly. In variations six and seven, there were three focal planes or main projected elements of the drawing. This may be illustrated by turning the viewing situation sideways and noting how a projection occurs:

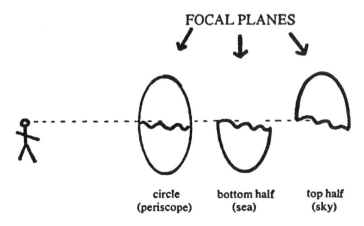

FOCAL PLANES

| circle | bottom half | top half |
| (periscope) | (sea) | (sky) |

This configuration interprets variation six, 3-d^{d-r}. It is possible now to project other possibilities according to where the elements of the drawing occur on all possible focal planes.

In a three-dimensional variation on the cameo variations, 2-d^{dr} and 2-d^{dl}, it is possible to move one focal plane element of the drawing to coincide with the focal plane of the circle itself, leaving the other open and thus distant in nuanced appearance, as diagrammed below:

FOCAL PLANES

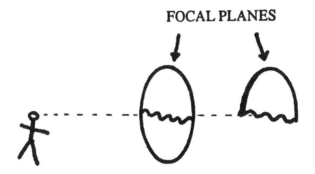

Its reversed appearance may also occur if the distant projected upper half replaces the bottom half, which rests within the circle as in the diagram. (Such variations would be eight and nine, respectively, and stories may be found to allow these variations to coalesce. For instance, suppose you are looking through a ship's porthole with a smudge obstructing the lower portion of the porthole. Then only the upper half is open to the outside and that outside is projected in the infinite distance, etc.) Each of these variations can be experientially fulfilled and have their own apodicticity.

It is clear now that a large number of topographical possibilities occur within the noema of a multistable drawing. Furthermore, if the essential insight into the types of multiple variations in such drawings has been attained, many more variations can be found in the previous figures as well. At this stage, students in the classroom are able to discern from two to four more variants on the Necker cube.

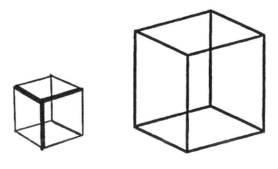

If, for example, the cube is seen not as a cube but as a hexagon, with two sets of intersecting lines drawn inside it, one set superimposed upon the other, it appears either as flat, with one set of intersecting lines dominant and the other set recessive (as in the heavier lines of the guide picture), or it appears as weakly three-dimensional, with one set of intersecting lines in front of the other (with reversals of dominant and recessive lines, and near and far lines, in the shallow three-dimensionality). The drawing and guide pictures above emphasize these features and should allow the variations to be seen.

Nor do these variations exhaust the cube's possibilities. However, two observations are now appropriate. First, the new variations are not as dramatic or as distinctive as the more obvious ordinary variations discovered earlier. The drama of discrimination has begun to take on a different tone. Once broken open, the ordinary sediment serving as the noetic background for vision recedes in significance as the extent of variations becomes known. The new appearance possibilities of multistable phenomena, at first strained and strange, become familiar and expected. I, for one, would be very surprised if I were not able to find polymorphy in a figure of this type that I had not yet investigated. Part of the secret of polymorphy has been penetrated, and so the subsequent variations become part of the work of refining what has already been attained in principle.

Second, as the extent of discernible variations is known, perceptual possibilities show themselves to be closer to conceptual, mathematical, and logical possibilities than has been thought. Once the elements of perceptual possibilities are identified, we can do something like a deduction of what will and what will not be fulfilled within perceptual experience. A process such as this was implicit in the circle example described. If the perceptual possibilities of dominance and recessiveness (figure/ground relations) can be combined with the projective possibilities of three-dimensionality, then we should be able to make an indefinite number of discriminations within abstract multistable drawings.

We now know that the field of perceptual possibilities is vast and complex, yet there is a structure and ordering principle to it. Thus, a new set of essential conditions emerges simultaneously with the breaking of the naive stereotype for multistable figures.

I shall not here elaborate all these conditions. Several have been alluded to in the last few pages. Noematically, for example, multistable figures contain possibilities for multiple arrangements of figure and ground, dominance and recessiveness, with respect to any given number of elements displayed. These elements may be projected in an indefinite number of possible arrangements with respect to the projective possibilities of nearness and distance in apparent three-dimensionality. Merely by combining such noematic traits, it becomes obvious that the number of possible combinations is large.

This is not to say that any conceivable combination is perceptually possible. The range of conceivability is probably much wider than that of perceptual possibility, even though the range of perceptual possibility is much more fluid and complex than ordinarily supposed. There are noetic limitations to perception, which derive from our finite bodily positions. For example, one noetic factor previously alluded to was the role of focus. Changing from wide focus to narrow focus can cause noematic changes (recall the curved-line example). Focusing on one part of a drawing can cause all the parts to arrange themselves around the area of focus and give a new and different appearance (this was part of the noetic device employed to turn the Necker cube into a two-dimensional insect). If this were a text in phenomenological psychology, it would elaborate these noematic and noetic features exhaustively and thus order the entire region of multistable perception.

It remains important to note that the explosion of the previously taken-for-granted phenomenon is nevertheless a contained explosion. The ordering process points to the limits of the phenomenon, the horizon of the multistable field. Horizons are by their nature indefinite and at the farthest extreme from what is clear and distinct, but they remain at least indistinctly discriminable.

A clue to the noematic horizon of the figures may be obtained from the relevance or irrelevance of the hermeneutic stories. Not just any story will do, nor will any empty possibility be fulfilled by looking at the figure. The hallway example does not let itself be seen as a swan flying. Only stories that free possibilities hidden in the configuration allow the gestalts to appear. Whatever the extent of the fulfillable variations may be, they remain dependent upon the *internal horizon* or limits that the drawing contains.

This horizon is a clue from which the structures of perception are reflexively learned. Corresponding to the relevance or irrelevance of the hermeneutic device is the structural limitation of perception. For example, the act of focus is extremely important in allowing a figure to appear as such and such a possibility. The psychologist Necker noted early that a shift of what he termed a point of fixation causes the cube to reverse its initial three-dimensionality.

The focus not only fixes some point, facet, or aspect of the drawing; it also serves as a value around which the other parts, facets, or aspects are arranged. Yet while focus has flexible and expandable variations, it does not have infinite variations, for two reasons. It is difficult, if not impossible, to focus on two widely separated facets equally and at the same time, which suggests something like a perceptual law of the excluded middle. And when focus takes in the entire visual field, everything in the field becomes less distinct and more distant (look into the distance and widen your focus to note this phenomenon).

This latter feature of perceptual activity may be taken as a sign of the directedness of intentionality in its full phenomenological sense. But before considering the significance of directedness of intentionality to the future development of phenomenological investigation, it is necessary to reflect on the process of inquiry that has taken place with the extremely limited set of phenomena examined in this book.

Summary: A Reflection Upon the Inquiry

The foregoing pages have offered an introduction to some of the tribal language of phenomenology and a preliminary working out of one set of limited examples to show the style of investigation and point up its implications for subsequent phenomenological investigations. No claim is made, even for the simplified and limited examples of multistable drawings, to either exhaustiveness or complete adequacy. Rather, I have tried to illustrate how one does phenomenology. A brief recapitulation of the stages of the inquiry will show the development of this method in capsule form before we extrapolate its significance for more complicated and profound investigations.

The investigation has been purposely cast in a Husserlian guise. This is appropriate for several reasons: Edmund Husserl was clearly the founder and originator of the method that became phenomenology, almost all major work done by the great phenomenologists has been inspired by Husserl, and it is my own conviction that while Husserl cannot have the last word about phenomenology, he must have the first word. The analytic mind at work in the Husserlian style of phenomenology must inform all phenomenological study and distinguish between phenomenology proper, hard-headed phenomenology if you like, from soft-headed imitators. Husserlian phenomenology moves step by step, makes fine distinctions, and solidifies each item before moving on to the next development.

All these attributes are not only in keeping with the dominant spirit of twentieth-century philosophy, but are also necessary if philosophy is to retain a rigor parallel to that of the sciences. Taking a single small region of multistable perceptual phenomena, I have outlined some of the major elements in a descriptive (and phenomenological) psychology—all of which can be seen to lead to even finer and more microanalytic investigations.

This is not to say that a step-by-step process does not become orchestrated into a recognizable movement. If we reflect on what happened over the span of examples investigated, the larger movement can be seen.

Take note of the more dramatic features of the phenomenological shift.

1. The first shift was what the Husserlian would call the deliberate shift from the natural to a phenomenological attitude. Those first given appearances of the examples used, seemed to have a certain familiarity, a naturalness, which was taken for granted and tacitly assumed to be *the* possibility of the thing in question.

On reflection, the Husserlian *epoché* is a device for breaking the bonds of familiarity we have with things, in order to see those things anew. But it is a device, because Husserlian phenomenological seeing has already placed itself outside and above naive seeing.

2. Phenomenological seeing deliberately looked for possibilities rather than the familiar, the taken for granted or the natural givenness of an object. Guided by this heuristic principle, phenomenological seeing pointed out strange possibilities—strange, that is, from the point of view of the sedimented and strongly held natural attitude. The first distinct perceptual possibilities appeared as dramatically different, surprising, and in some cases perhaps initially difficult to attain. This break with sedimented visual beliefs was necessary to clear the field for phenomenological, in contrast to empirical, investigation.

3. Once broken, the visual beliefs were reshaped so that a new level of familiarity emerged, the level of essential seeing, or eidetic investigation in Husserlian language. Now the sense of phenomena was opened, and their possibilities seen to be multiple, complex, and perhaps indefinite—limited only by the configurational internal horizons of each geometrical drawing. The sense of the phenomena changed, and the sense of seeing changed, both being open textured.

The diagram shows what is experienced in the change. The movement is a paradigm shift, which moves the investigator from one set of concerns, beliefs, and habits of seeing to another. It also contains a value claim that the new paradigm is better than the familiar one, at least theoretically and philosophically, because (1) new discoveries are made, (2) the previous point of view is shown to be inadequate in perceiving its field of phenomena and in its theoretical insights, and (3) it allows the development of a depth ordering of the new wider field of phenomena.

The diagram of this larger movement is:

[

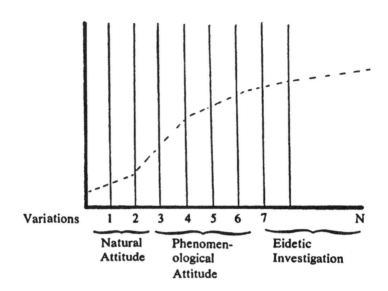

We have seen initially dramatic differences and distinctions discovered within the phenomena become a new, familiar (yet open) field for the development of distinctions and differences. If this movement were followed and consolidated, it would be possible to repeat the process with every multistable configuration. The new expectations (noetic context) are that the drawing contains n.... possibilities, and these may be actively sought out or elicited by the hermeneutic or the transcendental device. And while sometimes drawings will still display the standard empirical order, due to recalcitrant familiarity, increasingly, an arbitrary, although essential, order will replace it. Let each try for himself.

Projection

Expanding Phenomenology

The simple and abstract examples I have employed in this book pose two difficulties for the extrapolation of phenomenological method into weightier problems. One comes in part from the simplicity of the examples. They are reduced phenomena, nothing but bare lines on blank backgrounds. And although even these simple phenomena turn out to be far more complex than they are usually taken to be, they are almost too suggestive. Once the natural attitude is broken, their topographical possibilities emerge too easily. Also, their sedimented noetic context is shallow; they are thought of as games and puzzles. Our attitude to such phenomena, and thus the depth of our intentionality, is superficial. We might conclude that this phenomenology, which plays with puzzles, is merely an intellectual game, if somewhat more imaginative than most.

There is a playfulness in phenomenology, and the Husserlian emphasis upon the primacy of fantasy variations is a sign of this—but the playfulness is serious and has a purpose: eliciting structures or invariants. Ultimately, phenomenology claims that its method alone provides the adequacy needed for an ontology. But this raises a second difficulty. How is one to move from simple and abstract phenomena to more complex and "real" phenomena? And what does one discover in the process?

Here, I propose another Husserlian strategy, the use of approximation. If I assume that a groundwork has been laid in the previous simple phenomenology and extrapolate the method used to more and more difficult phenomena, the trajectory of the extrapolation should become clear. Of course it is not possible in the confines of a short introduction to do anything like a step-by-step analysis, but the following description shows the scheme of investigation.

The approximations I propose are (1) a phenomenology of material objects in the visual dimension, along the same lines as those noted in the line drawings; (2) a more complex aesthetic view of objects in the natural world, which suggests the lines of variant possibilities for constituting "worlds"; (3) alternative forms of vision in aesthetic traditions as an example of visual variants; and (4) a wider and deeper cultural variant, multilingual ability, which, I claim, exhibits isomorphism with the previous visual variants. All but the last of the approximations are visual and so the approximations fall short of a full existential phenomenology. I make a brief note of essential phenomenological elements in each approximation so the extrapolation suggests how and why most phenomenology eventually becomes an existential phenomenology.

First, material objects: Philosophers have not only been intrigued by ambiguous appearances; they have also spent great amounts of time and ink on the ordinary furniture of the world. Keeping to the visual, and with a deliberate approximation to the conditions surrounding multistable figures, it is possible to project perceptual variations into the realm of material objects.

Multiple perceptual possibilities for material objects have, in fact, been noted before. Illusions in the material world are not unknown and have been part of epistemology for centuries, but it is more important to this investigation to note that many standard psychologies are aware of reversal effects in material objects.

For instance, Ernst Mach discovered a depth reversal for a folded card viewed from above and from the front.[1] It can be seen as lying upon the table or it can be seen as standing on end. In principle this effect is isomorphic with the reversals previously noted. I shall leave it to the reader to discover whether further perceptual possibilities show themselves.

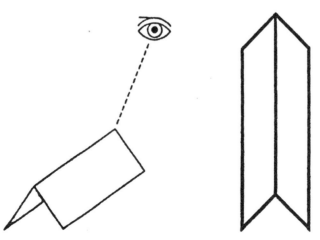

A similar effect is obtainable in a room the corners of which (preferably wall-ceiling corners of a plain-colored room) extend far enough out without connecting with other items. The point at which walls and ceiling intersect, normally seen as directed away from the viewer, can in reversed form be seen as directed toward the viewer.

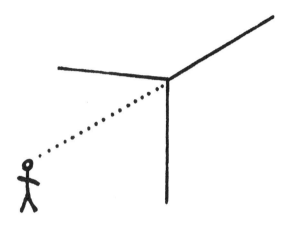

Examples can be multiplied and expanded along the lines of the previous investigation. Thus, multistable effects can and do occur with material objects. But in these cases there remains a certain oddness. First, such reversals and multiplications may be harder to obtain than for two-dimensional drawings. Second, the reversals are often harder to stabilize for long. Third, the object is believed not really reversed. Here there is a clue to a sediment deeper than that which displayed itself in the abstract drawings. In contrast to reversals in the drawings, repeated successes in reversal do not easily upset the privilege of one core variation.

If our examination of these reversible material objects is more closely scrutinized, several things come to attention. In both cases there is a remarkable similarity with the abstractness of the previous line drawings. Both are composed of plain surfaces uncomplicated by other configurations. Also, the viewer was directed to expect and ignore what is ordinarily seen, a type of viewing that is quasi-abstract, though directed at material objects. I shall contrast this type of seeing with what I call mundane seeing.

Mundane seeing is the involved, practical vision that characterizes most of our daily traffic with things around us. In the noetic context of mundane seeing, things are mostly use-objects or items of the environment. They are, moreover, charged with significance and not neutral, though they may be of little interest at any given moment. Some things may appear as threatening; others as beneficial and desirable; others as worth little note. Mundane vision is involved in a practical way with the surrounding environment, and the significance of what is seen occurs in that noetic context.

Abstract (including quasi-abstract) seeing sets aside the practicality of the mundane realm. It is directed to a specific theoretical concern. And that is its strength and its weakness—strength, in that, properly developed and trained, it discovers the previously unseen, weakness in that it can overlook the depth and implication of the involvement in mundane seeing.

Phenomenologically interpreted, abstract and mundane seeing are fundamentally isomorphic. They are both intentional in the deepest sense of the word, both are directed toward the surrounding world, and both have specific shapes reflexively derivable through phenomenological analysis.

Mundane and abstract seeing show two related shapes of intentionality. Both shapes are set in a full noetic context of beliefs, habits, ways of relating to phenomena—a sediment of ordered perceptual possibilities. Yet the simplified examples used for abstract seeing point up the difference between this and the more complicated and involved mundane seeing, and lead to the suspicion that whatever sediments are present in mundane seeing must be far more recalcitrant and binding for the viewer than those found in abstract seeing. This insight is the origin of the existential turn taken by most post-Husserlian phenomenology.

Existential phenomenology discovers and deepens the sense of intentionality by recognizing that even simple acts of viewing contain a latent stratum of praxical activity that ultimately implicates the very existence of the viewer. This latent stratum becomes reflexively more obvious if one imagines a variation upon mundane seeing. Suppose one sees a chair—there is a well-known illusion whereby parts of a chair are hung by nearly invisble strings, so that seen from the proper angle, the arrangement appears to be a standard chair, but from every other angle, it is seen to be a series of separate parts—which turn out not to be what it appeared to be. So long as this is a psychological experiment or an aesthetic trick, my involvement with the chair is minimal. But if I am to sit on the chair in an act that commits my body, it is much more important that the chair be what it appears to be. The very nature of abstract and quasi-abstract seeing makes this praxical element in mundane vision recede.

Existential phenomenology, with its emphasis on embodied or incarnate being (Merleau-Ponty) or being-in-the-world (Heidegger), takes this praxis stratum as basic. For existential phenomenology, seeing is seeing with one's whole body, because ultimately I commit my body through my mundane seeing. An existential turn does not deny the essential Husserlian discovery of the referentiality (directedness) of intentionality; rather, it recognizes that underlying the conscious and epistemological activity of seeing, there is a total directness toward the world on the part of the human knower.

The contrast between the disengaged, but still directed and referential seeing, and the engaged, mundane seeing, illustrates that the noematic and noetic constituents are more important, and hence more "real" in the domain that calls forth action, than in an act of abstract seeing. It is tempting to conclude that this is an index to phenomenological reality. For example, in the three-dimensional reversal of a material object, the "false" appearance seems to be a fringe possibility, and the "true" appearance the core possibility. Thus, a hierarchy of appearances can emerge, which is not so for the abstract possibilities of the line drawings.

However, a rigorous application of the phenomenological reductions precludes too easy or too early a conclusion on this matter, and the question arises whether a hierarchy correlated to praxical intentionality is the final word. Is praxical intentionality in mundane seeing analogous to the seeming naturalness of empirical order in the line drawings? And, if so, will it, too, relax its hold?

A fascinating aesthetic view of the world can be found in a farther-reaching set of examples. Carlos Castaneda describes one such difficult, but captivating example in the teachings Don Juan offers him. The old wizard advises Carlos to go out and look at a tree, and instead of seeing it in the usual way (the natural attitude), he instructs him to look at the shadows, so that eventually, it is the shadows that he sees as primary. The wizard is trying to get Carlos to reverse the dominant and foreground and the recessive and background, so that the ordinary tree/shadow appearance becomes a shadow/tree appearance, a shocking reversal.

I have tried this experiment and, with difficulty, succeeded in reconstituting the tree in this way. The effect is dramatic and startling. Here a living tree in natural surroundings suddenly shows a different and radically reversed perceptual possibility. (The experiment is interesting in itself, apart from the arguments surrounding Castaneda's work.) As might be expected, breaking the usual way of seeing is much more difficult in this case than in the case of the simple multistable figures. Yet, once accomplished, its impact and possible implications are much more important. While I am in no way interested in becoming a wizard, the possibility of a reconstituted "world" is, at the least, intriguing.

We can point to aesthetic shifts that have actualized perceptual possibilities in the history of several cultures. One such paradigm shift, revolutionary in its day, was made by the Impressionist painters of the late nineteenth century. To simplify, it might be said that one thing the Impressionists did was to look at light instead of at objects. Claude Monet's series of cathedral paintings, made at different times of the day, illustrate this point; the object in the paintings is the effect of different light on the cathedral, each painting revealing a different possibility of lighting. This shift in both noematic and noetic context was so radical in its time that the first viewers were said to be unable to identify the objects in the paintings.

A somewhat more radical shift occurs in a type of traditional Japanese art. In this art some object—a sparrow with a few blades of grass or a single cherry branch with blossoms—stands out against a blank or pastel background.

Our traditional way of viewing would say that the subject matter—what stands out and is dominant and in the foreground—is the sparrow or the blossoming branch. The background is merely empty or blank. This is entirely different from Western tradition in which the background is filled in. Yet the emptiness and openness of a Japanese painting *is* the subject matter of the painting, the sparrow or the branch being set there to make the openness stand out. In this, there is a radical reversal: the foreground is not dominant, the background is not recessive. To understand such a painting calls for a deep reversal in the noetic context.

It is not accidental that a similar understanding of the heavens pervades Japanese culture. In the early cosmologies of the West, the sky was the dome of the heavens, and seen as solid, its color was the color of the dome. In the East, the sky is the open and color recedes infinitely within the openness.

Although the cases mentioned above lack a full working out of a range of possibilities, they suggest what can be done and what can be expected through the extrapolation of phenomenological method. They follow a graded order, from the simplest and shallowest visual phenomena, to more complex and deeper ones. Most thoroughly worked out, abstract seeing was examined through line drawings of multistable objects. One step up, quasi-abstract seeing (in a restricted and isolated context) points out reversal effects in material objects. A further step up brought us to more complex, but still isolated, phenomena of the aesthetic order, which show how radical possibilities can be seen through artistic consciousness.

In each of these graded approximations of visual phenomena, the intentional phases can be noted. What is seen, the noema, is correlated to the act by which it is seen, the noesis. The noema occurs inside its field and only in relation to its field situated in its noematic context. Beliefs, expectations, and habits form the correlative noetic context. The series of approximations suggest that the more complex the thing viewed, the more difficult it is to break ordinary habits of viewing, the more recalcitrant the sediments. In short, the closer one comes to mundane, praxical seeing, the more difficult it is to achieve variability, which is the field for phenomenological investigation. Yet the same essential structure of intentionality pervades each level of involvement.

In these first approximations to existential phenomenology, as in the first moves of Husserlian phenomenology, what is learned about the existent or embodied being is learned *reflexively*. The involvements I have with material objects are "read from" the objects in their relation to me. Thus, while the abstract seeing of perceptual possibilities in multistable drawings is distant from deeper and fuller involvements, it nevertheless shows the general shape of involvement with objects. And the less demanding recalcitrance of the natural, empirical order of appearances, points to our deeper and much more recalcitrant world-beliefs and habits. Existential phenomenology takes these deeply held beliefs as its theme and examines the hold the world has on us and the hold we have on the world.

Graded levels of involvement suggest that all phenomena can show variational possibilities, and until these are uncovered, phenomenology cannot operate properly. But the deeper and more complex the phenomenon and the closer to the mundane it is, the harder it is to break with the natural attitude and see the variations. This is necessarily the case: the most familiar praxical activity has the most solidly packed and total sedimentation. This sedimentation constitutes a total cultural view, which is learned and lived from childhood on.

Perhaps the closest analogue to a total cultural view occurs in learning languages. A person who is reared hearing and learning a single language and later learns a second language, usually acquires that language slowly and painfully; he does not become fluent in it, and after a certain age, cannot learn it without a permanent foreign accent.

The stages of learning the language, too, are analogous to acquiring a genuine cultural variant. At first, one gropes, with insights coming in pieces and flashes. Often one must deliberately construct a sentence and mentally translate it to, and from, the primary language. Only after a long time does the second language come easily. Although learning a second language is slower and more difficult, it, too, parallels the process of gaining variations in multistable phenomena. One does not lose the apodicticity of the primary language, but it is seen to be but one way of "saying the world."

Another analogy with multistable phenomena is that once a second language is learned, subsequent languages come more and more easily. A further parallel occurs in that the different ways of "saying the world" in the second and third language seem dramatic and striking, but once the acquisition of language possibilities becomes familiar, this drama recedes and is replaced by a deeper understanding of the essential structure of "saying the world." Languages, in this sense, are profound ways of seeing the world.[2]

However, the language analogue is a much more comprehensive and complex phenomenon than the line-drawing examples worked out here. The infinite, yet structured, possibilities of natural languages are such, that a language may be a total view; the pervasiveness of language is such that its particular perspective is deeply engrained culturally and usually remains sedimented throughout one's life. Here, to my mind, is an essential reason why languages ought to be required for all higher education. To loosen the grip of the single view is a prerequisite for appreciation of varying views of the world.

The language example also makes the perspectival relativity implicit in variational theory apparent in a somewhat elevated way. Natural languages may, indeed, be considered the perspectives on the world of the people who speak them. I do not here wish to enter into the debate about whether a language determines the entire way in which we view the world (Whorf) or whether languages are so distinctive that radical translation is in fact impossible (Quine); but if one assumes there are internal focuses in language that help make the language distinctive, one can discern essential features of a linguistic perspective. To attain the essential features of a linguistic perspective, phenomenology would have to find the adequate variations. Of course, this would be no small task to complete for a series of languages.

Take a simple instance of existential-cultural relativity. That Eskimos have many words for snow; that the Arab languages have many words for camel; and that American English does not, is a well-worn point by now. A similar example emerges from recent history—American English is adept at creating new terms for technological artifacts, a tendency deplored by those who govern the French Academy. The result is that technological terms from American English now pervade French, both the technologists' tribal language and everyday speech. With technology goes language.

Clearly, multiplicity obtains if and when there are serious existential and cultural relations with an object. Skiers, who find it necessary to make more than the ordinary observation about snow, have caused some distinctions to be made (even in American English) for snow: "corn," "powder," "iced." Essentially languages can say what needs to be said, but the way in which they say it will vary widely and be related to a "form of life."

The relativities in these illustrations are commonplace, but the phenomenological point is the experiential and essential ground for why and how such relativities take shape. What is the ground for the often noted difference in time perception among the Hopi Indians and contemporary Americans?

This question does not arise unless the relativity is possible and appreciated. But once it is possible and appreciated, the range of variation and its deeper structure must be investigated. A phenomenological look at linguistic and cultural relativities goes beyond both assertion of cultural superiority (often made in extremely subtle ways in contemporary philosophies) and vacuous play among the richness of relativities.

If there is a depth structure of invariance, this is what must be sought through relativities. And this is the task of an informed phenomenology. The complexity of relativities point to yet another aspect of phenomenology in the future: to be informed, phenomenology must necessarily rely upon other disciplines. Its view of these disciplines, and particularly its interpretation of what they are doing, may be widely different from what those within the disciplines interpret their task and method to be, but without these other disciplines, phenomenology would be restricted to the realm of first-person experience. Intersubjective phenomenology is necessarily interdisciplinary phenomenology.

9

Interdisciplinary Phenomenology

Husserl's early and most optimistic view of the future of phenomenology was that all the sciences could and should be reconstructed along phenomenological lines. That at least some sciences could benefit from phenomenology has been indicated here in at least suggested form. For example, the empirical psychology of perception would be informed and opened to new directions by the essential science of descriptive phenomenology. Husserl held that an essential or eidetic science necessarily precedes an empirical science, and the discovery of a wider and deeper field of perceptual possibilities for multistable figures illustrates that there is such an essential level from which any empirical set of sediments might arise.

Once the phenomenological inversion has occurred, the wider field of possibilities is the essential one within which particular arrangements take shape. Not all fields of possibilities are arranged in the same way, as shown by a comparison between the investigation with multistable phenomena and the brief foray into similar occurrences with material objects. But all fields of possibilities display some type of topography, which becomes apparent only when the field itself is opened to the essential insight of the rigorously descriptive phenomenological look.

This Husserlian emphasis upon the primacy of the possible is the radical side of phenomenology and exemplifies its claim to be foundational with respect to the field of human experience. But there is another side to the issue of phenomenology and its relationship to the other disciplines. In the second half of the twentieth century, it is no longer possible for one person to acquire a large enough proportion of knowledge in every discipline, even to know what variations might be possible for a given domain of inquiry. For phenomenology to begin its investigation and critique of possibility fields, it must look to already constituted disciplines.

I have emphasized in this study the necessity of first-person experience in doing phenomenology—this is indeed the first word for phenomenology. Experiential verification is the second word, insofar as experiences reported by or taken from others must be scrutinized as possible, fulfillable experiences. But because the essential field is the entire field of possible experience, it is already in principle *intersubjective*, open to anyone willing and trained to follow the investigation.

The disciplines from which phenomenology must draw material for examination already contain latent insights and forms of variations that may be reinterpreted phenomenologically. The task is to discern what the leading problems are in relation to the framework that phenomenology, as a science of the possible, offers.

The connection of phenomenology with other disciplines is not original here. It has been pointed up particularly by the contemporary philosopher Paul Ricoeur. His "diagnostic" use of a whole span of disciplines in his own thought draws on the informative power of constituted disciplines, and his emphasis on the genuine otherness of the disciplines complements the less cautious claim of the earlier Husserl.[1]

It would be too ambitious and presumptuous, at the end of this book, to suggest a total reorganization along Husserlian lines. Moreover, to end with a system for applied phenomenology would breach the modesty fitting to a pragmatic American approach to things. But I shall note one phenomenological development in each of the main divisions of the disciplines. Where possible, I shall suggest a development in the general area of experience and its role in the sciences or arts. I am not suggesting that these developments are more basic or important than other phenomenological influences on the disciplines, only that they illustrate how one might deal with a problem in a discipline in a phenomenological way.

The Natural Sciences

From a phenomenological point of view, the natural sciences might be called noematic sciences insofar as their domains of objectivity are primarily concerned with object correlates. From their own point of view, noematic sciences may be little concerned with how a given field of inquiry relates to human intentionality. Philosophically, however, this concentration on noema can allow the correlated noetic questions to be overlooked. The question of how a given phenomenon is or may be made present necessarily leads in a philosophical direction. For phenomenology, the practice of science is a particular form of and development of human intentionality. Thus, one important question is how the observer is and can be intentionally related to a phenomenon; in contemporary scientific contexts this can be an exceedingly complex problem.

To observe implies some type of experiencing, and this experiencing in contemporary science is a question for the investigating phenomenologist. For the moment, I shall set aside three clearly important aspects of observation in the scientific context: seeing as it occurs within a community of technical discourse (itself strikingly different from ordinary discourse), the laboratory practices that are taken for granted in that context, and the relation of observation to predictive theory as such. Each of these problems is important and has been dealt with in the philosophy of science. Instead, I shall focus on some basic perceptual elements that are part of scientific observation. There is at least one analogy between scientific experience and phenomenological understanding of experience. Both deconstruct and transform ordinary experience. The scientist implicitly knows that intuitions are constituted. What he sees may be very different from what the uninformed individual sees, and this relates to the noetic context, which is quite differently and technically developed in science. It is necessary for both science and phenomenology to be able to take apart what is given so that its deeper strata may be discovered; in this, both transform what is taken to be intuitive.

The separation of scientists from the points of view of ordinary expectations leads to a different view of things and can cause problems. Today, the sciences tend increasingly to bring microphenomena into the center of interest. Particle theory and genetic theory are paradigm examples of disciplines concerned with microphenomena.

Observation of microphenomena, considered apart from the question of predictive theorizing, poses new problems for understanding what scientific observation perceives. Often scientists retain a strong sense of realism when dealing with microphenomena, but the more microscopic the observations, the harder they are to observe. Science asks whether or not there is an ultimate indivisible unit of physical reality. The companion question is whether or not there is a limit to observability. For example, particles are found by their traces; they are smashed at ultra high speeds into other entities, and the remains of these collisions are examined for traces. Here, ordinary perceptions are seemingly left far behind, and science is often tempted to hypothesize, in an ancient echo of the Greek atomists, that the smallest particles not only are impossible to perceive in fact, but impossible to detect in principle. At this borderline, the realism of the inquiry itself comes under suspicion, since it becomes difficult, if not impossible, to discern the difference between a purely theoretical (or imagined) entity and an empirical one.

Observations of this kind are made by means of instruments. Indeed, the more minute the phenomena, the larger and more complex the instruments.[2] It is here that an interesting set of questions can be raised for phenomenology.

What happens to and in perception when it occurs by means of an instrument? How is the perceptual intentionality of the observer mediated, and with what result? Such questions lead to a phenomenology of instrument-mediated perceptions as important for understanding how contemporary science situates its observations and its claims for its observations.

That such observations are still perception is clear enough. The scientist observes dial readings and tracings on photographic and computer-generated plates and, at least for confirmations of his theories, relates to a world through, with, or by instruments.

One phenomenologically oriented philosopher of science, Patrick Heelan, has argued that the use of instruments modifies perception substantially. He holds that the "worlds" constituted through direct or mundane perception experience and the "world" developed through scientific instruments are different, the ordinary "world" being constituted by ordinary perceptions and the scientific "world" being constituted by instrument-embodied perceptions.[3]

I have taken note of this suggestion in a somewhat broader context and attempted to consider what occurs when experience is directed through, with, and among technological artifacts (machines), of which scientific instruments are a subclass.[4] A few illustrations from this as yet preliminary development will point up the implications of instrument-mediated perception. In the quotations that follow, substitute "instrument" for "machine," and the point will be clear.

> I begin with certain simple experiences with machines and with the simple kinds of machines I can find. I pick up a pencil or a piece of chalk and begin to trace it across the desk or blackboard. Upon a careful examination of this experience, I suddenly discover that I experience the blackboard or the desk *through* the chalk—I *feel* the smoothness or the roughness of the board *at the end of the chalk*. This is, of course, also Merleau-Ponty's blind man who experiences the "world" at the end of his cane. If I begin to be descriptively rigorous, I find I must say that what I feel is felt locally at the end of the chalk or, better, at the chalk-blackboard junction. The "terminus" of my intentional extension into the world is on the blackboard, and I have discovered (contrary to empiricism) that touch is also a distance sense.

If I continue the reflection in terms of the phenomenological understanding of intentionality as experience within a world, I note that there is something curious about this experience. First, I clearly do not, in the case given, primarily experience the chalk as either thematic or as an object. Rather, what I experience is the blackboard and more precisely, a certain complex aspect of the blackboard's presence as texture, hardness, resistance, etc. I discern that I experience the blackboard *through* the chalk, the chalk being taken into my "self-experiencing."

By this I mean that the chalk is only secondarily an "object," while more primarily it is absorbed into my experiencing as an extension of myself. It is true, that the chalk is not totally absorbed in that I have what might be called an "echo focus" in which I feel simultaneously a certain pressure at the juncture fingers/chalk with what I feel at the end of the chalk. Nevertheless, in the primary focus it is the board which I feel.[5]

A phenomenological interpretation of what happens in one type of machine-mediated experience is shown in the next quotation, where I follow the same general correlational interpretation of noema-noesis, here called the human-world correlation.

This phenomenon may now be explicated in terms of the correlation model I have already noted. However, it is important to note where the machine is placed within the correlation. In the first case above, it becomes clear that the proper placing of the machine here must be upon the correlation line itself:

Human-machine → world.

The machine is "between" me and what is experienced and is in this sense a "means" of experience in the primary focus. Here, because the chalk is not thematized, it may be spoken of as a partial symbiotic part of the noetic act or of the experiencing of the noematic correlate in the world. This may be symbolized as follows by the introduction of parentheses:

(Human-machine) → world.

With this we have one type of human-machine relation, an experience *through* a machine. The correlational structure of intentionality remains, in that I do experience something other than the machine being used, and at the same time, my experiencing is extended through the machine for that intentional fulfillment. I may thus describe the chalk as having a partial *transparency relation* between myself and what is other. And in fact, the better the machine, the more "transparency" there is. Likewise, I can use a language now, which speaks of the machine as part of myself or taken into myself, so far as the experience is concerned.[6]

The machine- or instrument-mediated experience in which the instrument is taken into one's experience of bodily engaging the world, whether it be primarily kinesthetic-tactile or the extended embodiment of sight (telescope) or sound (telephone), I term an embodiment relation. These relations genuinely extend intentionality into the world, and when they operate properly, the sense of a new realism in the phenomenon can be retained. But this extension is not without other implications.

However, in such cases the transparency itself is enigmatic. It is clear that I do experience the board through the chalk, but it is equally clear that what is experienced is in some ways *transformed*. I do not experience the board through the chalk in the same way that I experience the board "in the flesh" with my own finger. Thus, when I compare my experience of the blackboard through the chalk and with my naked finger, I may note that in both cases I get a texture with its roughness or smoothness. But with my finger, I also get warmth or coolness, a spread sense of the spatiality of the board, perhaps also its dustiness or cleanness. There is a greater richness to the naked touch of the blackboard than the blackboard experienced through the chalk. I may now speak of the experiences of the blackboard through the chalk as a reduced experience when compared with my "naked" touch of the board.

Suppose, however, I replace the chalk with a finer instrument, let us say a dentist's probe made of stainless steel with a fine pick at the end. As I trace the probe across the board, I note more distinctly and clearly than before, each imperfection of the board's surface. Each pock mark or crack appears through my probe in an *amplified* way; perhaps even what I neither saw nor felt with even my naked finger becomes present through the steel probe. A microscopic presence is amplified through the probe, thus extending my experience of the board to a level of discernment previously unnoted.

In each of these variations in the experienced use of machines, I continue to note that the embodiment relation is one in which I do experience otherness through the machine, but that the experience through the machine transforms or stands in contrast to my ordinary experience in the "flesh."[7]

However, instrumentation that embodies perception is not the only instrumental possibility for perception. At a quite different pole of the correlational continuum a different possibility may be noted.

Suppose I investigate the basements of a modern university and I come upon a room filled with dials, gauges, rheostats and switches watched intently by a heating engineer. Suppose this control center monitors all the heating and cooling systems of the offices and dormitories. The engineer in the case "reads" his dials and if one creeps up, indicating that Quad X is overheating, he merely has to turn a dial and watch to see if the heat begins to turn to normal. If it does, all right, if not, he may have to call a building manager to find out what has broken down. Here the engineer is engaged in experiences *of* a machine.

Returning to our correlational model, this experience of a machine is curious. Through the machine something (presumably) still happens elsewhere, only in this case the engineer does not experience the terminus of the intention which traverses the machine. Thus we may model the relation as follows:

$$\text{Human} \rightarrow \text{(machine-world)}.$$

His primary experiential terminus is with the machine. I shall thus call this relation a *hermeneutic relation*. There is a partial opacity between the machine and the world and thus the machine is something like a text. I may read an author, but the author is only indirectly present in the text. It is precisely in such situations that Kafkaesque possibilities may arise (imagine that the heat dial has gone awry and in fact, when the engineer thinks the heat is going down, it is actually going up—or better, simply imagine registrars who relate more immediately on a daily basis to computers than to students). Of course, in these instances there is still a possibility of employing the difference between mediated and unmediated types of experience; the engineer could go to the dorm himself to note what was happening.

In some cases instruments probe into areas previously unknown where such checking is not at all possible, and in this case, we have a genuine hermeneutic situation in which it is the hermeneut who enters the cavern to hear the saying of the oracle and we are left to his interpretation. Thus, those instruments which probe the ultramicroscopic worlds of the atom leave room for doubt as to what precisely is "on the other side" of the machine.[8]

While this is very schematic, it points up an area in which a phenomenology of perception is relevant to an increasingly important problem in the investigation of microphenomena. Such a phenomenology ultimately ought to be able to outline the conditions of the possibilities of instrument-mediated observation and its attendant problems. But to do so in detail requires being informed by practicing the science itself. It is also a phenomenology that elevates a philosophy of technology to the level of importance now occupied by the philosophy of science, with its focus on the concept of theory.

The Social Sciences

If concentration on otherness in the noematic field leads to calling the natural sciences noematic sciences, social sciences might be termed noetic sciences, the reason being that the social sciences, notably sociology and anthropology but also history and some versions of psychology, concentrate on the field of constituted human meanings. The social, or human sciences turn to questions, in a phenomenological sense, that can be called questions about the origin, development, structure, and sedimentation of belief contexts as they impinge on human action.

Phenomenological work in the social sciences is probably better known and more thoroughly developed than in the natural sciences, and so there are a number of well-known phenomenologically informed sources. An early standard work was that of Alfred Schutz (see his *Collected Papers* and *Philosophy of the Social Sciences*, edited by Maurice Natanson), and a very recent phenomenologically oriented development has been the rise of ethnomethodology, led by Harold Garfinkel.

Between these two well-known phenomenological developments in the social sciences stands the work of Peter Berger and Thomas Luckmann, who have taken up the task of a phenomenological development of sociology and the sociology of knowledge. I shall briefly point out a few elements in their *The Social Construction of Reality* to illustrate how phenomenology operates as a noetic science in the social sciences.

Once the basic language and conceptual system of phenomenology is grasped, it is quite easy to make the transition to the technical language employed by Berger and Luckmann (more closely derived from Husserl and Schutz than the language used in this book). They, too, hold that philosophical, presociological considerations must be attended to before sociology can begin. "The method we consider best suited to clarify the foundations of knowledge in everyday life is that of phenomenological analysis, a purely descriptive method and, as such, 'empirical' but not 'scientific'—as we understand the nature of the empirical sciences."[9]

They consider the primary preliminary task of the social sciences to be the understanding of what and how the world of everyday life is constituted. In short, the descriptive task is an analysis of what is already sedimented and taken for granted, a phenomenology of the natural attitude.

> Among the multiple realities there is one that presents itself as the reality par excellence. This is the reality of everyday life. Its privileged position entitles it to the designation of paramount reality. The tension of consciousness is highest in everyday life, that is, the latter imposes itself upon consciousness in the most massive, urgent and intense manner. It is impossible to ignore, difficult even to weaken in its imperative presence. . . . This wide-awake state of existing in and apprehending the reality of everyday life is taken by me to be normal and self-evident, that is, it constitutes my natural attitude.[10]

What is here examined is the rise, structure, and constitution of a meaning-structure, the socially noetic state of everyday life.

Once the region of investigation is cleared, the description proceeds in typical phenomenological fashion. The range of experience in everyday life is seen to display itself in terms of a series of zones, which clearly approximate the focus-field-horizon structure elaborated previously in the multistable examples.

> The reality of everyday life is organized around the "here" of my body and the "now" of my present focus. This "here and now" is the focus of my attention to the reality of everyday life. What is "here and now" presented to me in everyday life is the *realissimum* of my consciousness. The reality of everyday life is not,

however, exhausted by these immediate presences, but embraces phenomena that are not present "here and now." This means that I experience everyday life in terms of differing degrees of closeness and remoteness, both spatially and temporally. Closest to me is the zone of everyday life that is directly accessible to my bodily manipulation. . . . I know, of course, that the reality of everyday life contains zones that are not accessible to me in this manner. But either I have no pragmatic interest in these zones or my interest in the far zones is less intense and certainly a less urgent field-fringe.[11]

Further, in a social noetic interest, a phenomenological sociology takes note of the intersubjective nature of the structures of everyday life. "The reality of everyday life further presents itself to me as an intersubjective world, a world that I share with others. This inter-subjectivity sharply differentiates everyday life from other realities of which I am conscious."[12] Here, the field of interest narrows to noetic, intersubjective phenomena and the isolation of the stratum of social meanings, the second of which has become the subject matter for phenomenological sociology. "Most importantly, I know that there is an ongoing correspondence between *my* meanings and *their* meanings in this world, that we share a common sense about its reality. The natural attitude is the attitude of commonsense consciousness precisely because it refers to a world that is common to many men."[13]

The problem for investigation, then, becomes the structure of reality of this natural attitude, of everyday life in its intersubjective constitution. Sedimentation occurs in the intersubjective noetic structure, and the processes of sedimentation are looked at phenomenologically. Berger and Luckmann see this process largely as occurring through tradition and through what they (following Schutz) term objectivation. Objectivation is the process of experience moving into language, which in turn is a social bond and institution of intersubjective meanings. Sedimentation and tradition, then, are the background against which empirical everyday life occurs.

What appears here is a new horizon structure (origins: real, constructed, lost, etc.) which limits the possibilities of a field:

Only a small part of the totality of human experiences is retained in consciousness. The experiences that are so retained become sedimented, that is, they congeal in recollection as recognizable and memorable entities. Unless such sedimentation took place, the individual could not make sense of his biography.[14]

Phenomenological sociology sees sedimentation as having an (immediate) experiential origin and being the genesis of objectivated meanings (taken-for-granted beliefs). Berger and Luckmann give the following simple example:

> For example, only some members of a hunting society have the experience of losing their weapons and being forced to fight a wild animal with their bare hands. This frightening experience with whatever lessons in bravery, cunning and skill it yields, is firmly sedimented in the consciousness of the individuals who went through it. If the experience is shared by several individuals, it will be sedimented inter-subjectively, may perhaps even form a bond between those individuals.[15]

This primary experience, shared by a few, can, however, be objectivated as a possible experience.

> As this experience is designated and transmitted linguistically, however, it becomes accessible and, perhaps, strongly relevant to individuals who have never gone through it. The linguistic designation . . . abstracts the experience from its individual biographical occurrences. It becomes an objective possibility for everyone, or at any rate for everyone within a certain type . . . that is, it becomes anonymous in principle, even if it is still associated with the feats of specific individuals.[16]

In this way objectivation leads to institution, ritualization, and the sedimentation of social possibilities.

Berger and Luckmann see this process happening primarily through language, which is the bearer of social sedimentation. "Language becomes the depository of a large aggregate of collective sedimentations, which can be acquired monothetically, that is, as cohesive wholes and without reconstructing their original process of formation."[17] When this happens, social sediment becomes an accepted, taken-for-granted belief that can lose or vary its justification. It becomes a static structure, a given, within social reality.

I shall not trace this analysis farther other than to say that, seen as a noetic structure, the phenomenology of everyday life and its sediments can go on to deal with such aspects of sedimentation as the necessary simplifications that allow sediment to be easily transmitted typifications, the way in which sedimentation becomes abstracted and ritualized, how it becomes equated with (social) knowledge, and is passed on from person to person.

Anthropological studies show many and various empirical constructions in human societies, and even variants within societies. What is of interest to a noetic science is the nature of the structure of sedimentation and tradition that produces these variants.

The Arts

The third set of disciplines to which an interdisciplinary phenomenology must relate are the arts, both literary and fine. Functioning as it does from a base of possibility fields, phenomenology is sure to find the arts a rich source, since they stimulate much creative imagination. The arts, taken as disciplines in which possibilities are explored and displayed for whatever motives (art for its own sake or for other purposes), practice possibility exploration and so have a profound relation to a central element and need of phenomenology. There is a deep relationship between artistic possibility exploration and possibility exploration in phenomenology which reveals the kinship between phenomenology and art. A phenomenological aesthetics, on which there has been some work, would surely view the arts as exercises in variations. The visual arts, for example, seek to explore the field of visual possibilities; music explores the auditory dimension; sculpture and architecture explore the spatial and material; and dance (and some sports) explores the field of bodily motion.

While not lacking noematic and noetic aspects, the arts, unlike the noematic and noetic sciences, exercise intentionality itself *as* variational. There is a playfulness in art deeply related to phenomenological playfulness, and it is possible to see the practice of the artist as latently phenomenological from the outset.

In actually exercising fantasy variations, the arts echo the Aristotelean dictum that poetics is ultimately more true than history. It is out of possibility that the undiscovered is found and created.

Given this relationship between phenomenology and art, it is no accident that almost every phenomenologist (at least since Husserl) has made some comment on the arts or made a more systematic foray into examining them. Martin Heidegger has examined poetry (*Existence and Being,* for example); Jean-Paul Sartre numerous literary topics (*Situations*), Maurice Merleau-Ponty visual art (*Signs* and *Sense and Nonsense*); and many others.

There have also been attempts to develop a phenomenological aesthetics and literary theory. Roman Ingarden's *The Literary Work of Art* and Mikel Dufrenne's *Phenomenology of Aesthetic Experience* stand out.

But to comment on phenomenology and art at a more basic level, the level at which the variational richness of art emerges, is to look at the activity of imagination. Imagination has been a theme of many phenomenologists, but one of the most systematic works has just appeared: *Imagining: A Phenomenological Study,* by Edward S. Casey.

A phenomenology of imagination spans all the arts and isolates an essential intentional dimension in disciplines that strive for a display of possibilities. Casey's analysis is cognizant of this aim and its profound relationship to phenomenology. His thesis, which emerges from a concrete, descriptive study of the imagination, is that the imagination is uniquely autonomous, though initially he characterizes this autonomy as thin.

> Recognizing the thin character of imaginative autonomy vis-à-vis other denser types of autonomy may help us to understand why the autonomous action of imagining has so often been questioned—or simply bypassed—by previous investigators. It is as if they had asked themselves the following skeptical question: How can an experience so tenuous, so fragile and fleeting as imagining be autonomous? Overlooked in this question is the possibility that imagining's very tenuousness may provide a clue to its mode of autonomy. Perhaps imagining is autonomous *in its very insubstantiality.*

But what then *is* imaginative autonomy? The answer to this question may be encapsulated in the following two statements:

1. The autonomy of imagining consists in its strict independence from other mental acts, from its surroundings, and from all pressing human concerns.

2. The autonomy of imagining consists in the freedom of mind of which imagination is uniquely capable.[18]

This phenomenology of imagination shows, in contrast to many previous theories, that the role of imagination is an irreducible function of intentionality. Its autonomy, the autonomy of the multiplicity of intentional acts, is one irreducible role of mind.

> A recognition of the multiplicity of the mental—a multiplicity that is borne out precisely by the existence of eidetic differences between various kinds of mental acts—must replace a vertical view of mind if we are to avoid the harmful consequences of thinking in exclusively hierarchical terms. It is only within the mind's multiplex structure that imagination's autonomy has its place—a place

which, however singular it may be, is not rankable as topmost, *or* as bottom-most, *or* as middlemost.[19]

This seems like a modest claim for imagination. It is thin and but one of a group of mental activities. Moreover, Casey argues that the imagination per se is not necessarily creative in either the artistic or unartistic sense. "[T]*here is no inherent or necessary connection between imagining and being creative; they are only contingently connected.*"[20] However, according to Casey, the thin autonomy of the imagination has a unique role. It is the intentional activity that opens the field of pure possibility.

> *Pure possibility*, finally, is the thetic expression of imaginative freedom of mind. Even if the purely possible is subject to certain formal and practical limits, these ultimate boundaries are not nearly so constrictive as those imposed upon whatever is empirically real. Pure possibility enables the mind's free movement to traverse a terrain considerably more vast than the region occupied by perceived and remembered things alone. . . . Each journey into such a domain is potentially endless, since a given series of pure possibilities has no fixed terminus. Here freedom is the freedom of never having to come to a pre-established or peremptory end.[21]

Possibility as such arises from imagination, Casey claims, because it is the nature of imagination to vary itself. Variations are the very life of imagination.

> In the present context such multiplicity assumes the specific form of *variability*, that is, the mind's freedom to vary itself indefinitely and without end. . . .
> Variation means multiplicity; being a variation upon something else, a given variation always implies *other* variations, actual or possible. Consequently, a mental act whose basic operations continually engender variety will be free in the special sense of giving rise to multiple options, directions and routes.[22]

Thus, in spite of his very moderate claims for imagination, admitting its thinness, its lack of either inferiority or superiority over other mental (intentional) dimensions, Casey ends up seeing in imagining a link to human freedom.

> To be free in this fashion is to realize freedom of mind to the fullest. For the human mind thrives on variation, even as it seeks

unification; and imagining, more than any other mental act, proceeds by proliferation: it is the primary way in which the mind diversifies itself and its contents. Mind is free—is indeed most free—in imagining.[23]

Without detracting from Casey's conclusions, I take exception to locating freedom solely in the imagination. Multistable phenomena as well have opened the way for finding variations and possibilities within perception. Accepting the recalcitrance of variations in perception, linked as perception is to the basic praxis of bodily life (in contrast to the floating freedom of the imagination), it remains the case that every dimension of intentionality displays a possibility field.

However, imagination, with its freedom to dissociate, to place imagining far from mundane concerns in its own natural *epoché*, brings variability directly and immediately to the fore. Most prosaically, infinite variability of imagining may be seen in its spontaneity and its capacity to be continued indefinitely without regard to constraints. "Just as we are only rarely coerced to imagine in the first place, so we are almost never obliged to proceed in accordance with what we have already imagined."[24]

It has already been noted how essential the capacity to vary things is to phenomenological philosophy. Casey sees the same capacity as essential to the arts.

> The possibilizing activity of imagination in art opens up an experiential domain which would not otherwise have been available, either to the artist or the spectator. This domain is one in which *everything appears as purely possible*. Within the medium bound, spatio-temporal limits of a given work of art, the domain of the purely possible emerges whenever imagining is functioning autonomously.[25]

The realm of the possible, opened by imaginative variations, is the common ground of the arts and phenomenology—each according to its respective purpose.

> It is imagining *as autonomous* which introduces the factor of pure possibility into aesthetic experience. Only an autonomous imagination can project, explore and populate the domain of the purely possible in art. This domain is intrinsic to the very being of works of art, and yet it is left unaccounted for in representationalist and expressivist theories, both of which fail to appreciate the autonomous

activity of imagination in artistic creation and enjoyment. . . . In art—whether in making or contemplating it—we not only perceive or feel; we also imagine, thereby entering a realm that would otherwise have remained closed to us.[26]

Multiplicity, variation, pure possibility: this is the region in which a healthy art and a rigorous phenomenology can and must play. Whether this region is thin, as Casey holds, or the ultimate source of discovery of both the real and the irreal, as Husserl held, phenomenology and art are kin.

Yet the genius of phenomenology, which makes it so different from its nearest of kin, binds its playfulness to a desire to create new sciences. Only through variation, Husserl claims, does the invariant show itself; only through phenomenology is a fundamental ontology possible, claims Heidegger. Neither of these claims concerns the arts; but they are essential to phenomenology. But this is merely to say that art is not philosophy, and philosophy is not art, even though an artful philosophy is to be preferred to any other kind.

Part II

Pragmatism and Postphenomenology

10

Pragmatism and Phenomenology

Edmund Husserl and John Dewey were born in the same year, 1859, and by the beginning of the twentieth century both were innovating two of the most radical "philosophies of experience" to appear, *phenomenology* and *pragmatism*. By 1905, now more than a century ago, Husserl was giving his lectures on internal time consciousness, and John Dewey had just started his famous laboratory school. And although Dewey lived longer than Husserl, 1952 and 1938 respectively, and did most of his major work a bit later than Husserl, the two twentieth-century philosophies were destined to change the face of late modern philosophy.

We are entering, just now, the century-later phase of the high points of early phenomenology and pragmatism. I propose in this chapter to look at both phenomenology and pragmatism with glances at their heritages and then propose that their mutual concerns could well be newly productive, in this now century-past context, by becoming a *postphenomenology*.

Both phenomenology and pragmatism began, in a very broad sense, as philosophies of *experience*, but with a whole series of complementary sub-themes as well. Much of this territory has been well explored: from pragmatism, Husserl drew much from William James as is well known and deeply explored by Bruce Wilshire in his *William James and Phenomenology* (1968); other pragmatists, such as C. S. Peirce, were influential for structural phenomenology as Elmar Holenstein showed in *Roman Jakobson's Approach to Language: Phenomenological Structuralism* (1976); G. H. Mead relates to much of Alfred Schutz's work and what became the "social construction of reality" in Berger and Luckmann, which, in turn, had impact in the new sociologies contemporary "social constructionist" movement. Rather than explore these works, however, I want to focus upon what could be called the postclassical movements of phenomenology and pragmatism.

The subcultural settings for phenomenology and pragmatism differed. Husserl worked in the culture of the German universities, conversing with his colleagues and related to his cognate disciplinary interests—logic, mathematics, epistemology. His descriptivism, his interest in ideality and theory, his mathematizer's view of science, all echoed the dominant intellectual strands of the early-twentieth-century German research university. In the United States, Dewey's two primary appointments were in what were considered to be at that time, "experimental" universities: the University of Chicago, and later Columbia University. This was particularly the case with respect to views upon education. Dewey's Laboratory School reflected this experimentalist culture in his setting. These settings were those of the early twentieth century in which phenomenology and pragmatism were initiated.

I want, however, to look more closely at the respective heritages that follow this formative period, with particular emphasis upon the American scene. "Classical" pragmatism had its immediate Dewey proponents among Dewey's colleagues and students. In their own time, both Dewey and Husserl had colleagues and collaborators who developed philosophy along pragmatist and phenomenological lines close to the founders: Joseph Cohen, Samuel Levin, and John Donahue come to mind with Dewey and Ludwig Landgrebe, Alexander Pfaender, and Adolf Reinach associated with Husserl. Still it is the later post-founder period that interests me here.

If we are looking at heritages, we need to be careful to distinguish several kinds of heritage: there is a *scholarly* heritage, by this I mean interpreters of, expositors of, and perhaps appliers of a founder. Then there is a *praxical* heritage, that is, a following that borrows practices and key notions of a founder but carries these out in either a new setting or to different purposes. The first, the scholarly heritage, is more historiological; the second, the praxical, is more adaptive. What I have in mind is clearer with respect to pragmatism's outcome in America with Dewey, than, perhaps, it is with Husserl.

Dewey was adopted, mid-century, by the leading group of American *analytic* philosophers, who rather than doing Dewey scholarship, took Deweyan practices into their own work. I have in mind Willard Van Orman Quine, Donald Davidson, Wilfred Sellars, and Hilary Putnam, the "postanalytic" gang forefronted by Richard Rorty in *Philosophy and the Mirror of Nature*. He showed how analytic pragmatism was nonfoundational, nontranscendental, anti-Cartesian, and, although now situated in a style of philosophy that centered itself on logic and linguistics, was pragmatic. This thesis was pushed farther in his *Consequences of Pragmatism*. The outcome, I would contend, is that Rorty's analytic pragmatists could just as well be called *postpragmatists*.

Carl Mitcham, himself a pragmatist, has pointed out that one salient feature of pragmatism, going back to Peirce, is the shift from a representationalist belief epistemology to an actional or practice-oriented analysis, in pragmatism: "[B]eliefs were more properly interpreted as habits of acting than as representations of reality, and thus not so much in need of special foundations as being located in historical and social processes."[1] But I shall follow, for a moment, Rorty's characterizations: "My first characterizaton of pragmatism is that it is simply anti-essentialism applied to notions like 'truth,' 'knowledge,' 'language,' ', morality,' and similar objects of philosophical theorizing."[2] The fall of prior distinctions follows and relies upon the shift from beliefs and representations to the recognition of practices within human culture and society. "The pragmatists tell us, it is the vocabulary of practice rather than theory, of action rather than contemplation, in which one can say something about truth."[3] This shift implies the nonfoundationalism found in the transcendental traditions: "So pragmatists see the Platonic tradition as having outlived its usefulness. This does not mean that they have a new, non-Platonic set of answers to Platonic questions to offer, but rather they do not think we should ask those questions anymore."[4] Thus, Rorty's characterization of pragmatism, which continues to work itself out in "conversations," albeit conversations clearly retain the focus of what he earlier called "the linguistic turn" in analytic philosophy.

I shall not here trace step-by-step what I take to be the parallels to phenomenology, or to its own early complementary movement in Husserl's thought. His own uses of Descartes and Kant, although reflecting off each, effectively inverted each and I would contend ended up in the actional-focused *genetic phenomenology*, which my colleague Donn Welton has argued for in *The Other Husserl*. Even more, the echoes of a historically, praxically oriented analysis such as occurs in the *Crisis* and "The Origin of Geometry" brings Husserl even closer to what I have described as pragmatism.

Rorty, of course, continues to hold that Husserl and phenomenology are "idealist" and foundationalist. "I myself would join Reichenbach in dismissing classical Husserlian phenomenology, Bergson, Whitehead . . . as merely weakened versions of idealism."[5] Is Husserl a foundationalist? If his phenomenology is *transcendental*, then in some sense he retains some variant of foundationalism. I am quite aware that this issue remains one of keen interest within contemporary Husserl scholarship, as does the issue of whether or not Husserl should or should not retain some version of Cartesian subjectivity. Stephen Crowell, for example, has argued in "The Cartesianism of Phenomenology" that some version of Cartesianism *should* be retained by phenomenology. That debate, however, I do not wish to enter since my program here is more prescriptive than expository.

What I am after with the formula "pragmatism + phenomenology = postphenomenology" comes from a recent observation made by Carl Mitcham. Mitcham, as many others, has remarked upon the critique of phenomenology that its *descriptivism* tends to make it blind to, or difficult to propose normative issues—ethics, politics, social issues do not seem to be a phenomenological *forte*. In his contribution to *Postphenomenology: A Critical Companion to Ihde*, Mitcham has been looking at what I call *postphenomenology* with particular focus upon technoscience and pragmatism He notes, "The challenge *to* pragmatism is to consider what . . . a phenomenology of human-instrument relations might imply for pragmatist instrumentalism. The challenge *from* pragmatism is to consider in what ways . . . phenomenology might be a basis for societal, political and technological reform."[6] That is, could there be some kind of *hybrid* of phenomenology and pragmatism that could be equally robust in description and yet sensitive to normative or reformist developments? It is this possibility which I suggest may have implications for a *postphenomenology*.

To accomplish this goal and give a perspective, I shall return to a theme from my article, "Husserl's Galileo Needed a Telescope" (*Philosophy and Technology* 24, no.1 [2011]). There I argued that Husserl's philosophy of science was too embedded in early-twentieth-century views, which saw science primarily as a theory-biased, mathematization process without sensitivity to science's embodiment through instruments, technologies. I shall here take up that same thesis in a different way, a way that indicates simultaneously how close Husserl came to a pragmatist insight, yet how far he remained, due, in part, to his vestigial, but recalcitrant "Cartesianism." As remarked earlier, Husserl rarely commented upon technologies or instruments, but two of his most salient remarks and examples come from the *Crisis,* and in particular "The Origins of Geometry." And it is in these works that hints of how close he comes to pragmatism—even to a possible *nonfoundationalism* that would be open to what I am calling "postphenomenology."

I am going to very succinctly follow three themes relating Husserl to pragmatism: *historical-cultural origins; the focus upon praxis;* and the role of *instruments*. In each case I shall parallel Husserl to pragmatism.

The Historical

Recall, first, early pragmatism, repeating the above cited Peircean claim, "[Knowledge is] more properly interpreted as habits of acting than as representations of reality, and thus not so much in need of special foundations as being located in historical and social processes."[7] Husserl's *Crisis* and "The Origin of Geometry" present a version of a unique type of the "historical." He argues that the geometry that Galileo used to invent early modern science was handed down, taken for granted, but its "origins" lay back in a history with a tradition of being both handed down and developed. Thus, one has to "question backward" if one is going to recover the originating act by which geometry appears.

With respect to geometry, Husserl proposed a historical questioning backward:

> "[W]e must . . . inquire back into the original meaning of the handed-down geometry, which continued to be valid with this very same meaning . . . and at the same time was developed further. . . . Our considerations will necessary lead to the deepest problems of meaning, problems of science and of the history of science in general . . ."[8]

Husserl contends this historical back-questioning is *not* philological-historical, or a search for actual inventors or originators. "Rather than this, our interest shall be the inquire back into the most original sense in which geometry once arose, was present as the tradition of millennia, is still present for us, and is still being worked on in a lively forward development."[9]

It is, in short, a historical—dare I say "hermeneutical"—phenomenology of the origins: "[T]here is an inquiry back into the submerged original meanings of geometry as they necessarily must have been in their 'primally establishing' function."[10]

And, Husserl recognized that this historical questioning-back was quite different from the—and his—usual epistemological styled inquiry. "Certainly the historical backward reference has not occurred to anyone; certainly theory of knowledge has never been seen as a peculiarly historical task. But this is precisely what we object to in the past."[11]

While I, myself, believe this shift to the historical, a questioning-back, may likely echo Heidegger's "destruction of the history of metaphysics," which so much of the post–*Being and Time* discussions and debates between Heidegger and Husserl evidence, the point is equally relevant to a *lifeworld phenomenology*, which explicitly highlights history, culture, and traditions, all of which Husserl discusses in "The Origin of Geometry." The parallelism with the pragmatism cited above is also obvious.

Praxis

What is to be phenomenologically analyzed in this historical questioning back? The answer is, and examination of, *practices out of which origins occur.*

Joseph Cohen, a Dewey contemporary, claims, "Out of technical processes and slowly accumulating skills, out of combinations and recombinations of the tools and expertise of many peoples came the eventual theoretical organization of technology into science."[12] Here is a pragmatist perspective on practice originating science, or in our context, practices leading to a "geometry." But what practices? Husserl's claim, both in the *Crisis* and "Origins" is *measuring practices*. I shall not fully lay out Husserl's complex *Crisis* analysis here, but merely highlight some features that bear upon the measuring practices as parallel to pragmatism:

> Phenomenologically, humans live in an actional, perceptual world where "[W]e experience 'bodies'—not geometrical-ideal bodies but precisely those bodies that we actually experience, with the content which is the actual content of experience."[13]
>
> But, Galileo already had at hand an ideal geometry, which was already a "tool" to be applied. It was an ideal, but lifeworld-available "tool." But because of this, Galileo could "forget" that this tool was acquired. "It will be instructive to bring to light what was implicitly included in his guiding model of mathematics, even though, because of the direction of his interest, it was kept from his view: as a hidden, presupposed meaning it naturally had to enter into his physics along with everything else."[14]
>
> We know that Husserl's view of this acquistion was one in which actual measurements suggested "limit shapes" beginning with simple shapes such as straight lines, squares, triangles, and the like, each gradually perfected and then "idealized" into the objects of a "pure" geometry. "We can understand that, out of the praxis of perfecting, of freely pressing toward the horizons of *conceivable* perfecting 'again and again,' *limit-shapes* emerge toward which the particular series of perfectings tend, as toward invariant and never attainable poles."[15]
>
> Thus, it is from the practice and art of measurement that geometry originates, but once made "pure" or "ideal" it can then become a conceptual tool for further development. This, then, leaves us with a concrete, material world of plenary objects and an idealized world of ideal objects. For Galileo this double is a process of "coming into contact with the art of measuring and then guiding it, mathematics—thereby descending again from the world of idealities to the empirically intuited world—showed that one can universally obtain objectively true knowledge of a

completely new sort about the things of the intuitively actual
world . . ."[16]

Thus, through the analysis of *praxis*, here measuring practices, Husserl generates the "origins of geometry," which function differently for Galileo than for the originators and thus produce the
"crisis" that can arise by forgetting origins, or now understood,
the praxical origins of this particular science. Mitcham's way of
putting this for Dewey is that he "argued that the methods of
the sciences broadly construed—including technology—serve as
distinctly human tools in a human lifeworld that is continuous
with a larger non-human lifeworld."[17]

Instruments (Technologies)

We are here left with a tension—Husserl is claiming that Galileo's lifeworld
is bifurcated insofar as Galileo can use a "pure and ideal" mathematics, which
indirectly applies to the equally taken for granted plenary, bodily world, but
the application "forgets" its origins, which we have located in measurement
practices. Measurement practices, however, use *instruments*, *tools*, or as we can
say, *technologies*. It is precisely these that are "forgotten." We now reach my
own claim and critique concerning Husserl and pragmatism. Mitcham repeatedly notes that for Dewey "there is no difference in logical principle between
the method of science and the method pursued in technologies."[18] There is a
sense, within pragmatism [and predating Heidegger] that technology carries a
"sense broad enough to include science,"[19] or, put in my terms, science cannot
be separated from the lifeworld insofar as it is an instrumental, technologically
embodied practice.

The problem for classical, or, Husserlian phenomenology lies in its
insensitivity to precisely this problem. Husserl rarely deals with technologies,
materialities, except as fully plenary perceptual *objects*. Here is a clue to his
vestigial *Cartesianism* as well. It is as if the world were primarily that in which
an ego comes in contact with objects, "out there, passively received objects."
Husserl, in this sense, remains in strong contrast to Heidegger's claim that
we first encounter "tools" in praxical contexts and that objects in the above
sense, appear only after a rupture or breakdown in our everyday practices. But,
in our context here, the late *Crisis* and "Origins" Husserl comes closer to the
recognition of the role of technologies. For my purposes here, I shall, again very
succinctly, examine one example of Husserl's—*writing*—and one example he did
not use from the history of measuring practices—Egyptian geometrical practice.

Writing

"Origin" is one of the few examples of some detailed analysis of a technology or instrument developed by Husserl. And even this analysis is a kind of "in passing" illustration in the context of how objectivities are intersubjectively constituted in the history of geometry. Nevertheless, writing entails materiality, instrumentality: "The important function of written, documenting linguistic expression is that it makes communications possible without immediate or mediate personal address: it is, so to speak, communication become virtual. Through this the communalization of man is lifted to a new level."[20] This is a new recognition, that through a technology, writing, communalization can be lifted to a new level. I would and have argued that the same is true for instrumentation in science.

Here, however, we have the technology of writing. Husserl presupposes some kind of text, a written-upon page, with subsequent examples such as newspapers. (Again, I cannot refrain from commenting that much of what follows echoes quite closely Heidegger's rants concerning *das Man* and *Gerede* in *Being and Time!*) It is when he begins to analyze reading that the troubles arise: "Written signs are, when considered from a purely corporeal point of view, straightforwardly, sensibly experienceable; and it is always possible that they be intersubjectively experienceable in common."[21] That is, there are marks on paper, intersubjectively experienceable. But, Husserl introduces a second description: "But as linguistic signs they awaken, as do linguistic sounds, their familiar significations. The awakening is something passive; the awakened signification is thus given passively, similarly to the way in which any other activity which has sunk into obscurity, once associatively awakened, emerges at first *passively* as a more or less clear memory."[22]

Were I to rephrase this, here is what I think is going on: We come upon a piece of writing, a printed page. At its purely sensible level it is "markings on a paper." But, if we take it up to read it, we must "re-activate" its linguistic signification by an act (such as a memory act, Husserl claims). *Pardon me, but I think this is vestigial, but pure early modern epistemology, both Cartesian and Lockean!* Primitively, there are the bare qualities—here, marks on paper—to which must be added or recalled meanings. No wonder then that this "technology" leaves us in precisely the ideality/lifeworld split that characterizes Galilean forgetfulness. And Husserl confirms this: "There is a distinction, then, between passively understanding the expression and making it self-evident by reactivating its meaning. But there also *exist* possibilities of a kind of activity, a thinking in terms of things that have been taken up merely receptively, passively, which deals with significations only passively understood and taken over, without any of the self-evidence of original activity."[23] This returns us to the search for origins recommended earlier by questioning-back. For writing, this recommendation is thus one of hermeneutic character and must be seen as *active*.

I propose to counter what I see as vestigial early modernist epistemology in Husserl's analysis, by redescribing the situation:

> Phenomenological variations upon writing: First, I come upon a newspaper; second, wandering in the desert I come across a broken tablet—a stele—with writing upon it; third, I check my e-mail. First, *in none of the cases does some bare set of qualia show itself; to characterize each in such a way would call for an act of deliberate abstraction, reductive of what shows itself, the thing itself.* Although still "bare" objects, the emphasis in the *Crisis* recognizes *plena,* or multisensory, plenary objects. But even this is not enough since, I would agree with Heidegger and Merleau-Ponty, all "objects" come as already significant in particular ways. In my three variants, all show themselves from themselves as styles and types of "writing," seen as "writing." In the first case, the newspaper, it is immediately English, familiar and ready to be read. Yes, I can do an "origins" analysis, since the entire process is familiar from reporters, news services, editorial practices, and the like. In the second case, even if the language is both unfamiliar and possibly antique—say, Aramaic—it is recognizable as script and calling for reading, which is not yet fulfillable. To do an origins analysis here calls for more elaborate practices, those related to linguistics, archeology, and the like. In the third, e-mail case, the script is almost like conversation, but recognizably script in any case. If it is immediate, an origins analysis might even be a conversation-like e-mail exchange. I have, in fact, been very curious about this perception of writing as a script-like phenomenon and have tried a number of perceptual variations to try *not* to see written artifacts as scripts. I contend that it is not easy to do this! And while I have not concluded my exercises, it has become possible to do a bit of foreground/background inversions, which allow one to see a densely printed page, not as writing, but as a series of foreground white patterns against a black background of somewhat indistinguishable dark patterns—but so far I have to squint or deliberately de-focus for that to occur.

Negatively, I am suggesting that even in this rare instance of dealing with an instrument or technology, Husserl retains the vestigial epistemology that still divides realities into something like bare material objects and something else like a meaning-giving subject that constitutes meaning, whether by activation or reactivation. His version of an origins search, while clearly pointing to an analysis of practices, overlooks the role of materiality in the process. Thus, one can return to my three writing variants and do a somewhat different origins analysis:

> In each of the cases, the written result (newspaper, stele, email) has been produced. The product itself incorporates this process and, I would say, displays this from itself. Bruno Latour claims that speed bumps incorporate administrators, policemen, and builders. Similarly, written objects incorporate in a material form all the accumulated practices of whatever writing practices were at hand when the newspaper, stele, or email were produced. And when one "reads" these with whatever degree of background capacity, those features are "perceived" in the artifact. This is better and deeper than the eighteenth-century deists, who argued that if one finds a watch on the beach, one may infer a designer. But phenomenologically, we should not make the mistake of saying that finding some pattern in nature implies a designer since the natural pattern is recognizable as quite different from the stele in the desert. The pre-given significations of sedimentation patterns on the White Cliffs of Dover are quite different from the watch on the beach.

Phenomenologically, one is supposed to let the "things themselves" speak. But "first speech" is not what is claimed in what Descartes and Locke mean by bare qualia, which are highly reduced and abstracted qualities.

Egyptian Measurement Praxis

My second example returns to Husserl's own question concerning the origins of geometry. From today's perspectives, Husserl can perhaps be forgiven for his decidedly Eurocentric views. He argues that geometry is one geometry and that once discovered, something such as the Pythagorean Theorem simply repeats itself but remains *one*. And, since his history is itself something of an ideal history, it may make no difference to him that the so-called Pythagorean Theorem has been discovered and put to different uses in at least six different ancient cultures (see Dick Teresi, *Lost Discoveries* [2002]). And, I argue, had Husserl's idealized questioning-back also been informed by a more mundane historiology, he might have actually gained some satisfaction in what it shows. Assuming that if geometry arose from measurement practices in line with Husserl's claims, the question emerges as to what these practices were, for example, among the ancient Egyptians. Here is what I have discovered:

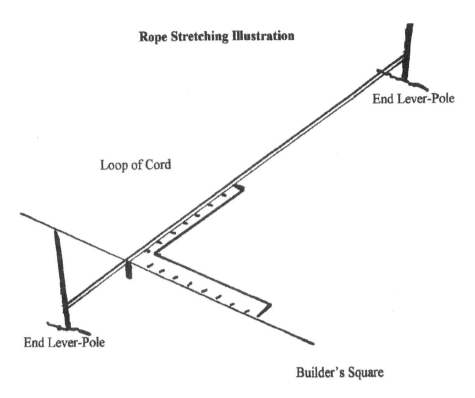

Figure 10.1. Egyptian Rope Stretching.

Egyptian civilization depended upon a stable infrastructure that related to the annual floods of the Nile. But these floods, while agriculturally beneficial, also wiped out the boundary markers between fields—these had to be reestablished on an annual basis. In Vermont, we actually have an office called the "fence watcher" that is an elected individual who cares for boundaries and disputes between owners. The Egyptians pre-dated this and their geometrical practices which reestablished the field boundaries between owners, did so by means of surveys with *stretched ropes*. This practice is reflected in the actual notation for their mathematics—"1," "10," and "10 squared" are rope signs.

Number Examples

1   10   10'

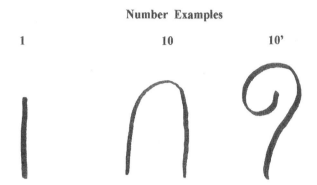

Figure 10.2. Egyptian Rope Style Numbers.

The Egyptians also employed a very practical device, which yielded a version of the square of the hypotenuse or Pythagorean Theorem in field boundary practice. Let us take brief note of the rope-stretching practice: I have here redrawn a depiction of the goddess of writing and measurement, Sheshet, as she assists a Pharaoh in the ritual of "stretching the cord," part of the measurement practice that sets everything from field boundaries to pyramid foundations.

Figure 10.3. Rope Stretching Ritual.

While this practice is simple—indeed, it was a rediscovery for me that the way I set straight lines for garden planting, by string stretching between two poles, was an echo of an ancient practice—it was the means by which a practical geometry worked for reestablishing fields, or, for that matter, for outlining straight sides for pyramid or temple foundations. What Husserl would have liked is precisely this set of *approximations*, ever approaching limit-shapes, but at this stage also limited to quite simple shapes (straight lines, pyramids, pillars, squares, etc.). And, one could also speculate that this kind of nonideal history might please Husserl because it does suggest that the tradition remains open to development. Egyptian geometry—for that matter Greek geometry—never developed geometries for complex shapes. For example, the compound curves common in ship building never had a geometry of use until nineteenth-century geometries—but ships of elegant form were built anyway, well before the nineteenth century. But, what was handed down? In Husserl's account it is essential that the step toward idealization, towards a "pure" geometry be made and then that is what is handed down. The concrete practices that produced and suggested the ideal were what presumably dropped away.

Or, are there other possibilities? One such possibility is that the attainments of ancient geometry were resituated *in a different set of practices, practicing geometry, as it were.* To oversimplify, if rope-stretching surveyors could go about producing straight lines, squared fields, pyramid blueprints, could not these same straight lines and shapes be taught in a different practice? Could the resultant straight lines and shapes be taken up by students of geometry, who could then "apply" them to yet other practices. Could these new practices, now reembodied in drawings, and taught in proto-academies be a very way for a resituated tradition to be transmitted? Let me revert to my first Husserlian example, the phenomenon of writing, to illustrate more related to this possibility.

There are many, many examples concerning the origins of writings—and I am deliberate with the use of plural—which show that many styles of writing begin with a notation that is pictographic and only gradually move toward something much more *abstract*. Again, this would not be out of line with the Husserlian trajectory. I have previously shown some of these examples in *Technology and the Lifeworld*.

Figure 10.4. Pictograph to Lettering.

Here, the phonetic development of what is today our letter "A" is shown to have been derived from an earlier pictograph for Aleph, the Bull. Or, in Chinese, what was more a pictograph of a boat becomes in late Chinese the multidimensioned phoneme, ideograph, or fragment for other ideas and words. Is this a movement from concrete to abstract, from materiality to ideality? I do not think so. Instead, if one goes to the actual practice of writing, what happens is that there is an inclination to speed up the process. Detailed pictographs simply take more time and effort than letter "A" or ideograph "boat." In short, here we have a human-material process or interaction such that, in carrying out a project through a developing technology, one produces new and previously both unknown and unused capacities of human-material processes. Husserl himself, perhaps unconsciously, exemplified this: he used and developed an idiosyncratic shorthand for his manuscripts which have bugged Husserl scholars ever since.

I am suggesting that if Dewey was right that there is no difference in logical principle between the method of science and the method in technology, and if technological practices are understood broadly enough to incorporate science, then a pragmatically enriched phenomenology, a *postphenomenology*, might be, like Husserl's origins of geometry, a further development in phenomenology itself. I have tried to demonstrate that at least the late Husserl comes closer to pragmatism, both of which begin to forefront practices, history, culture, and tradition over the metaphysics of foundations earlier favored in modernity. It is this shift from representationalist epistemology, combined with a sensitivity to both praxis and materiality, that I term *postphenomenology* with the title formula: phenomenology + pragmatism = postphenomenology.

Part III

Material Multistabilities

11

Simulation and Embodiment

Technology Plots Persist

The topic here is simulation and human embodiment. While there are all sorts of simulations, ranging from modeling processes through the now-pervasive computer tomographies, to imaging technologies, I shall be focusing upon the relationship between the human user and "reader" of these simulations in action. In this chapter I have chosen three distinct, but related, trajectories of simulation technologies, and will analyze these with respect to human embodiment.

First, however, I want to situate this analysis in a somewhat broader and often more implicit background phenomenon. I have long been struck by what could be called two interrelated traditions of interpretations of how we humans develop and use technologies: technology plots. The one tradition is utopian and exemplifies a set of desires and imaginations that sees in technologies ways to get beyond our human limitations through creating machines which give us previously unknown, but wanted, powers. Such dreams and desires are doubtless as ancient as humans themselves, and they were often expressed in fantasies of technologies—magic carpets that fly, cloaks that protect from weapons or that make one invisible—but in antiquity the magic helpers were just as likely or more likely to be animal—flying horses, giant birds, or even genies in bottles. Interestingly, in the late Middle Ages, these fantasies began to more and more image technologies as the means for increased powers—Roger Bacon's submarines and flying machines, later drawn by Leonardo da Vinci in his technological imaginations, and up to contemporary dreams for virtual powers such as those imagined by William Gibson in *Neuromancer*.

The opposite set of plots, plots that worry about what such powers might do to us, are dystopian in form and are variations upon the theme that humans reaching beyond their set powers endanger themselves: Icarus flies too close to the Sun; Faust enters a Devil's bargain; the Golem; Frankenstein; and on down to Terminator—all become human-invented nonhuman beings who turn upon us.

As these persistent plots mutate and modify over time, they nevertheless persistently display existential themes that reverberate with our hopes, fears, and desires relating to our technologies. On the one side, these plots display our fears—if we invent technologies that challenge the gods or exceed our humanity, we are tempting fate or endangering our humanity. Here, our technologies are cast in a *dystopian* light and we fear being overcome by our own creations. Yet, on the other side, we want our technologies to enhance our limits and give us powers we do not have. Here, the *utopian* hope is for our technologies to give us what we lack.

But, ultimately, both the dystopian and utopian fears and hopes often hide the mirror images each have of the other. Because each displays the technologies used in these fantasies as being simultaneously both different from and yet the same as ourselves. When placed in the context of embodiment, these contradictory desires are of special interest—we both want and do not want full embodiment. But, all of this is merely the instantiation of the existential contradiction in the desires we have concerning our technologies: we both want the powers we are not, and do not, have, and which we dream our technologies can give us, and yet we want those technologies to be so transparent that they become our very selves, what we are, and thus we find ourselves in the contradiction of both being and not-being one with our creations. I note this background before turning to the current focus upon simulations. What is it we seek in simulations?

Simulation

To repeat, the topic is simulation and embodiment. It is a topic that often gets situated precisely within the parameters of the contrary plots I have just outlined, at least in popular culture. The plots form the cultural background for the technological development, which inhabits the foreground. Simulation, sometimes popularly linked with *virtual reality*, is hyped as a technological substitution for "real life," later, "augmented life" or even "hyperreality," which will, when fully realized, be able to challenge or even replace the mundane "real life" that we now experience. Such claims, always based upon slippery slope arguments, engage both the utopian and dystopian plots mentioned. The utopians see in virtual reality, fictional means of fulfilling desires not possible within the limits of our present experience, and dystopians fear for the dissolution of "real life" into fantasies that will threaten "human nature" itself. I shall assume the reader is quite aware of this situation given the often full press of discussion of cyberspace, virtuality, bodies, which fills much of what occurs over the Internet, the media, and even to some extent the more popular science publications such as *Scientific American.*

My own approach will be more mundane, and definitely more phenom-enological. And, it will take as the sometimes hidden but always present variable of human embodiment as its fulcrum for the analysis to follow. My thesis is that human embodiment forms a sometimes explicit, but always at least implicit variant for technologies, including those used in simulations. I will develop here three trajectories, all of which reflexively point to human embodiment from within the simulation technologies. I shall begin with a trajectory that follows added sensory dimensions for its effects; then a trajec-tory that locates points of view [popularly POVs], and finally a trajectory of visual hermeneutics, all related to simulation and embodiment.

Trajectory One: Adding up Perceptual Dimensions

Example #1. Early and Recent Cinematic "Realism"

Cinema, or "movies," are relatively recent examples of simulation technolo-gies. In the very early days of movie experimentation, the Lumière brothers, developed what became known as *cinema verité.* Indeed, on of the most striking examples was their short *L'arrivée d'un Train en Gare de la Ciotat* sequence, which showed a steam engine entering the station. The camera was placed so that the train seemed to come right down upon the virtual spectator position and when shown, reports indicated that the audience screamed and jumped as they reacted to the virtual "realism" of the scene. Motion, new to the viewers, was enough to suggest a new kind of film "realism." Skip now nearly a century to a contemporary IMAX virtual and 3-D "realism." My own first experience of IMAX was in Japan in 2000, and I was watching *Echoes of the Sun.* One scene shows sugar molecules floating around, some of which came directly at me in full, glowing color, 3-D effects, and sound-enhanced motions—I admit to having jumped a little at the first surprise. I reacted not very differently to my first experience of IMAX than early cinema viewers did to the *Train en Gare.*

Now take a time-variant between the two events. When I first saw the *Train en Gare* clip, I did not jump. The now antique-appearing movie seemed merely artifactual and curious, and it seemed strange to me that viewers would have taken it as virtually "real." Clearly, the technological distance was quite large, from grainy black and white, soundless film, one could say "monosensory" since it was a visual only, to the richer audiovisual, full color, enhanced surround-sound, and three-dimensional IMAX, in which the "degrees" of virtual realism had certainly been enriched.

But before drawing any premature conclusions, allow a bit of phenomenological analysis: First, I take it that insofar as embodiment is a concern, phenomenology gives priority to what might be called "whole body activity." This is to say that we humans are multidimensioned perceptually; that kinesthetic-sensory actions are primary and implied in all our activities; and that this is the basis for what we take to be our opening or relation to any "real" environment. In my examples, however, the virtual "realities" of the train entering a station and the molecules flying in my face, are highly *reduced* realities.

By taking account of variations between the presented phenomena, this distance between imaged and non-imaged is clear: In the case of the Lumière train, the imaged train is black and white, displayed within the frame of the screen, lacks all the dimensions of sound, smells of the smoke, etc. Compared to being in an actual train station, it would seem that this highly reduced-image train is quite different from the fully embodied experience. Any reflective, critical approach should be able to show that. Yet, the early viewers reacted strongly to the imaged arrival of the train. The technological development from 1895 to 2000 and IMAX shows an enrichment of virtuality: the sugar molecule coming to my face appears 3-D, is colored and dimensional, is located within a soundscape, and is fully audio-video, and, like the early Lumière viewers, I reacted. But, and this is important, this was my first—and I will call it a naïve—experience of IMAX. Later, in fact in the same movie, I had learned to be more critical. The molecules flying at me remained reduced—they had no tactile presence, if I raised my hand the very image was blocked, etc. And, without the goggles, the whole illusion disappears.

The situation I am describing is a very complex one, but my initial point is that the technologically mediated situation is one that displays distinct differences between it and the ordinary, whole body engagement with non-imaged phenomena. The difference between Lumière and IMAX is one of degree only. The situation is also complicated by the need to straighten out the differences between naive or first or early experiences of the novel situation, and later, more critical ones of the "same" situations. In short, there is both a statics and dynamics that need to be taken into account.

And, there is also a need to take into account the social or cultural context within which the simulations are taking place. My examples above are from entertainment contexts, which are designed to enhance precisely the novelty, the startling naive experiences I have described. One enters theatre-space along with a willingness to suspend ordinary expectations. The shock effect of Lumière or IMAX quickly dissipates with repeated viewing; one does not jump or twitch with later expected anticipations. Only the critic is likely to come back to do the more precise analysis and learn more from the structuring of the show. Frame-by-frame analysis is done within what Paul Ricoeur calls a "second naivete" approach. In Ricoeur's hermeneutics, first naivete is like the simple belief a religious person might have about biblical texts, taking them as literal accounts of things. A "second naivete," however, is an informed and critical return to the text in Ricoeur's sense, after one has learned of the historical, cultural, archeological, and other dimensions that went into shaping the text.

A similar effect may be noted as both the technologies and the genre matures. The change is quite marked between the contemporary viewer's take on early, compared to more recent, horror film genres. Viewing early "mummy" movies today seems quaint, even though many of the same tricks of surprise with some bizarre object—the mummy—are replaced with the distorted masks of the "Scream" series.

This same movement from a first to a second "naivete" also occurs in scientific discovery, but not by design. Examples: Galileo's "aha" with his first sighting of Jupiter's satellites; Roentgen's "aha" experience with his discovery of X-rays and the first image of his wife's ringed hand; Watson's "aha" with Rosalind Franklin's X-ray crystallograph of DNA structure, are all examples with some parallelism to my Lumière and IMAX experiences. In each of these cases, some new phenomenon was recognized within a gestalt instant. But, in science as in film criticism, what follows in "second naivete" may be as, if not more important than, the initial "aha."

Example # 2: Flight and Military Simulation

In my first set of examples there was an implied trajectory concerning what I shall now call perceptual *isomorphism* and virtual "realism." That trajectory moved from the reduced, visual motion isomorphism of the Lumière example, to the enriched audiovisual, 3-D isomorphism of IMAX. But both are far short of the norm of ordinary, whole body experience of an environment found in mundane life. Yet, this reduced trajectory is suggestive—could simulation be even more virtually "realistic"? Historically, this trajectory has also been followed and developed in simulations that attempted to increase virtual isomorphism. I have in mind specific training simulators such as those developed from early flight simulation to the present pilot training simulators of the present.

Although as early as World War I it was recognized that fighter pilots, if they survived the first five flights, were likely to survive much longer, pilot training aids did not function well. But Edwin Link patented his Link Pilot Trainer in 1931. It pitched, rolled, dived, and climbed, and even had a feedback mechanism to give the controls "feel." It was a smaller replica of an airplane into which the trainee would enter. It moved according to the controls and had a full instrument panel. But at first the military was not interested and so Link sold his models primarily to amusement parks. But, after a series of accidents—five deaths in the first days of flying air mail—the Army Air Corps did buy Link Trainers and soon these were being used primarily to train for night and instrument flight. The Link Trainer "simulated" this type of flight. Indeed, it was for instrument or blind flight that the trainer was primarily designed. Then, with World War II, thousands of improved models went into production and all Army Air Force cadets took blind flying instruction from Link Trainers.

One can see here that virtual simulation had now taken another step in perceptual isomorphism. To sight-motion, and to full audiovisual motion, kinesthetic and tactile dimensions were added. Today, flight simulation is standard, not only for the military, but for commercial pilots. My ex-daughter-in-law, a 747 pilot for United Airlines, has to regularly pass simulation exams that present her with crisis situations never likely to be encountered, but for which she is trained. These simulators are much more "realistic" than the earlier Link Trainers. Full visualization of airports or outside scenes are displayed on the windscreen; sound effects and motions are also included and users indicate that the crisis situations they have to respond to make them sweat and tremble during use. Researching this topic on the Web, I also discovered that simulation programs for restricted areas—New York, Washington, D.C., etc.—are now prohibited! Simulation training was, after all, part of the training undertaken by the suicide pilots of 9/11. Note an interesting irony here: perceptually isomorphic simulation in early flight simulation was primarily useful in perceptually restrictive situations—blind or instrument flight. But today's simulators produce much more isomorphic and multi-perceptual dimensions in their effects. Yet, in each case, a second naivete is one that must recognize that all such simulation is *framed*, one enters it within the special limits of the tasks assigned. Just as the early advertisements for the Link Trainer noted: no one has ever died as a result of a simulated air crash, any more than anyone has ever been hit by an IMAX sugar molecule. Moreover, simulation today precedes the contemporary long-distance actual control of robotic aircraft. The Predators that fly over Pakistan and Afghanistan, are flown by users stationed in simulation-like control rooms in Nevada, U.S.A.

Trajectory Two: Points of View (POV)

Example #1: Embodied and Disembodied Positions

Although many philosophers, not only phenomenologists, have noted that we always experience the world from an unstated but reflexively locatable *perspective*, this becomes particularly interesting in simulation technologies. R. D. Laing, in his *The Divided Self* (1965), described two points of view often noted when persons describe how they experience an environment, the "embodied" and the "disembodied" positions. I have developed this distinction more fully in my *Bodies in Technology* (2002), noting that only in the embodied position does one have the full, multidimensional perceptual awareness of an experience from a situated position. For example, in a long practice when teaching phenomenology, I asked students to describe some experience they would like to have, but in fact had never had. It turned out that some variation upon flying was the most usual and even dominant example they would choose (Icarus remains with us!). When this was made concrete in examples such as parachute jumps, I noted that two types of descriptions emerged: most described the imagined experience in "embodied" form, that is, they would describe jumping from the airplane, the vertigo in one's stomach, the feel of air on one's face, the rushing appearance of the ground as one fell, the jerk of the chord with the parachute opening. But others, at mid-century, usually a minority, described the experience in "disembodied" form, that is, they would see themselves jumping from the airplane—which was "up there"—and see themselves as bodies falling, etc. In further questioning, it became clear that the "disembodied" form was at best "mirror-like" and called for an identification of myself with some image of myself falling "over there." Yet, the relationship between "embodied" and "disembodied" perspectives is also such that the "embodied" implied that position from which the "disembodied" is taken. It is interesting to note, however, that the majority/minority ratio changed over recent decades with more recent polls bringing the classes into more equal embodiment/disembodiment ratios.

Turning now to my first simulation technology, video games, such POVs are often depicted in the displays of game variants. Here, for example are three such variant POVS:

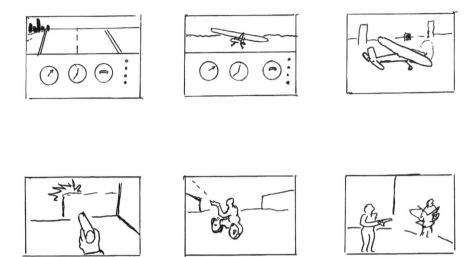

Figure 11.1. Computer Game POVs.

In the first column the player is presumably in embodied position, the gun being held out as if from one's bodily position, or the instrument panel as from one's seated position. On the far right, the disembodied position is depicted and one must make a silent assumption that "I" am in the airplane over there, or that "I" am the person sneaking up on the victim. Interestingly, video games often now employ a sort of hybrid position, with the "I" or avatar, is in a near or "piggyback" position. I am here closer to the projected "I" of the also displayed disembodied figure, but still disembodied "out there."

Example #2: Imaging Technologies and Apparent Distance

I shall not here follow too deeply the implications of embodied perspective, although I would note that they may be found in all imaging technologies and may be phenomenologically recovered in such phenomena as "apparent distance," which accompanies all isomorphic displays. The history of telescopy shows this trajectory quite dramatically. Here is a series of illustrations to show how *apparent distance*, that is, the distance between the observed object and the implied observing subject, decreases with technological development.

Figure 11.2. Telescopic Apparent Distance.

This series shows the dramatically decreased apparent distance between the viewer and the astronomical object being viewed. From Galileo's early depictions of the satellites of Jupiter to present satellite imaging of now easily recognizable entities such as Saturn's rings. In these cases, the displayed view implies a position of the observer, but does not display that POV. Embodiment remains an invariant, but in this case it is reflexively implied in the phenomenon of apparent distance. At the same time, note that while this type of isomorphism retains its embodiment's reflexive reference, that reference is also a highly reduced one compared to the first trajectory noted. Here, I have reverted to the monosensory, visual display, which leaves in the background the other perceptual engagements with the world. The implied bodily position is thus located in a sort of image-produced *irreal* position which reduces the full range of motility, multdimensional perception, and, in short, the primacy of action called for in the mundane world. Yet, there is also a gain: by mediating that which is not—at least at this point in our history—available to an actual bodily presence, the diminished distance of apparent distance produces an appreciable epistemological gain. My point, however, is that embodiment remains an implied invariant even here.

And, before leaving this trajectory, phenomenologically the common use of "apparent" distance is also questionable since it implies a kind of "realism" not phenomenologically accurate. A better term, to my mind, would be *relative distance*. The distance actually experienced by the telescope viewer is the closer distance which the mediating technology makes possible. "Apparent" distance implies privileging a nonmediated situation in which the "real" distance between the viewer and celestial object is that which is measurable from a third-person or ideal observer position.

Trajectory Three: Visual Hermeneutics

Example: Imaging beyond Bodily Capacities

I now come to the last of my three trajectories, this one finds its place in a relatively new set of capacities of imaging technologies. The technologies I have in mind here are those which, since the mid-twentieth century, have simulated or presented phenomena that lie, strictly speaking, beyond the ordinary and perceivable capacities of our human bodies. The first example lies in the new imaging, now common, in astronomy. Up until mid-century last, all astronomy was limited to optical or light-frequency imaging. But with the development of radio, and then radar technologies, astronomers gradually became aware of celestial radiation that lies beyond optical ranges. Radio astronomy, which soon yielded radio sources as well as the cosmic background radiation, began to open astronomy to new phenomena entirely. Celestial radio sources, in many instances, did not correspond to optical sources.

Although two modes of imaging were first used—auditory radio sources could be heard as a hiss on radio equipment—it was not long before the cultural practice of science to visualize, was also employed and visual displays of radio sources were also imaged. But I want here to cut to the quick: for a visual display to be produced, one has once again to imply human embodiment. That which lies beyond perception is made perceivable—in the visual display. Today, what is often called the "new astronomy" displays a whole range of emissions, from very short gamma rays through very large radio waves, far exceeding the narrowness of the optical range previously available to sighted humans with telescopes.

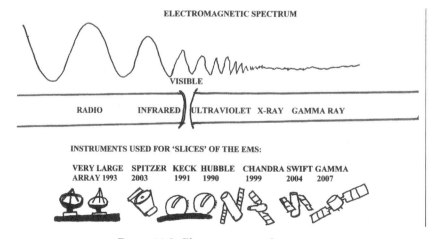

Figure 11.3. Electromagnetic Spectrum.

With the discovery of the microwave spectrum, it became possible to design instruments that could image various "slices" from that spectrum. Today's "telescopes" can image radiation sources from gamma rays to radio waves, with each yielding previously unknown (and unexperienced) phenomena from X-ray, ultraviolet, radio, frequencies etc. And, while I have used astronomy to open this imaging-simulation revolution, one can find the same style of imaging in the medical and most other sciences. Particularly popular today are brain scans that utilize different imaging technologies such as CT X-ray, PET, MRI, and fMRI scanning machines.

I want to take quick note of these new imaging technologies with respect to their simulative capacities. First, what I have discussed are mostly "slices" of some imaged object from which different frequencies or images from different molecular processes produce narrow band images. These can also be combined to produce variants upon 3-D or composite images. This is done through computer tomography, which can synthesize or produce composite results. All of these processes are no older than the mid-twentieth century and many are new to the twenty-first century, thus amounting to an imaging revolution which is now already taken for granted.

But, where in all this, is embodiment? It is, as in my second trajectory, *implied*. But this time it is implied as a human visual perceiver. Within the science context I have used in this trajectory, the visual display for human perceivers is what constitutes the embodiment situation. But to make this work, scientific visualism must become *hermeneutic*. In the two series of "slices," from astronomical to medical, the images are those which are technologically constructed from data to display gestalt patterns visible to the human perceiver. There is thus a double *translation*, the first from data to visual pattern, but also from pattern to—in my examples—*false color displays*. (And I have the same phenomenological problem with this now standard terminology that I had with that of "apparent distance." "False" color, implies a "true" color, which in this case would be precisely a "color" impossible for us to experience since it lies beyond our bodily range. I here again prefer *relative* color, in this case relative to our hermeneutic purposes.) Once this is done, a trained and critical human observer can then do the embodied action of seeing at a glance the various configurations that reveal the significance of the display. Human perceptual capacities are thus brought into play and embodiment is indirectly at work, or better embodiment is being mediated through the enabling imaging technologies.

Strictly speaking, of course, what is being perceived is precisely what cannot *without technological mediation* be perceived. The simulations thus give voice or make visible what in mundane situations could not be heard or seen. Thus, once again, it is precisely through the highly reductive process that the transformation occurs into the humanly perceivable, which makes this simulation epistemologically valuable. But it is also the case that this complex set of transformations and translations implicitly takes into account human embodiment.

Plotting the Trajectories

One of the tasks for philosophers is that of locating patterns. That is what I now want to do by plotting the three trajectories against the phenomenological notion of embodiment I am using. The position I have been taking is consonant with those of the earlier philosophers, the later Husserl with his mediations upon *Leib*, but even more with Merleau-Ponty and his notion of *corps vecu*. Both recognize that human embodiment is complex, multidimensioned, located in the intentional, directional arc of motility, perceptually rich, and that the motile body is the necessary condition for intelligent behavior and our "opening" to the world.

What I have done is to have added the technological dimension, which transforms and translates our embodiment into our reach through instruments, in this case imaging and simulation instruments, thus into what we can experience and know of the world. It is against this backdrop that the three trajectories I have traced show some interesting patterns.

First, in the trajectory that began with monosensory simulations and then increased its complexity of those dimensions, adding audiovisual to visual, and ultimately kinesthetic-tactile to audiovisual, one could see a trajectory toward, although not reaching whole body, motile experience. The simulation technologies remain short of full bodily, mundane experience. Yet, there are two different directions that are interesting. First, even with the reduced monosensory Lumière example, viewers jumped as the train pulled into the station. The "aha" phenomenon was one of motility faced with the virtual motion of the train. My account of this relates to the primacy of bodily movement as the core of embodiment—even apperceptively we respond, at least with first naivete, to motions that appear theatening. But, the second and critical direction is also to be noted. Even with the most sophisticated and multidimensional simulations, one remains short of mundane experience. Bodily motion is either restricted or in the background. In the theatre, either Lumière or IMAX, one remains seated, and even with the most complex virtual reality engines, such as those with gloves and goggles, one's motions are in-place motion. This is part of the theatre-like *framing*, which gives a clue to virtuality rather than the mundane.

The second trajectory, even more than the first, forefronts something like a stationary or reduced bodily motility. Perspective, or POV, in theatrical, game, or imaging contexts favors reduced bodily motion. The player is relatively stable with limited motile movements in front of the screen. While embodiment is indeed implied, it is quite locally positioned. In the phenomenon of *apparent distance*, while there is an apperceptive dimension, it remains within the context of the technological framing situation. Thus, in the second trajectory again, there remains a distinct difference between the framing of the trajectory and mundane motility. (I am not here addressing the Wii and subsequent game and other technologies, which push farther than the station-location of games toward a more motile practice. But such a trajectory is consistent with those noted.)

In the third trajectory the features just noted for the second are also maintained. But in this case it is the world correlate that calls for attention. And in this trajectory the difference between a first and second naivete is of great importance. To "read" the images calls for an explicit awareness of the transforming and translation processes. The false colors reveal, but reveal in a distinctly mediating mode. I must take account of my perceptions within a hermeneutic process.

Yet, in all three trajectories, embodiment remains the invariant to which the displays are addressed. Embodiment is not necessarily foregrounded, and thus may not be obvious, but even when backgrounded, it can be seen to be what provides one set of constraints for simulation development. My contention is that by making embodiment thematic and by taking it into critical account, we are more likely to be able to develop more interesting and innovative simulations. But, equally, I am also contending that we cannot actually escape our selves, our bodily selves in this development.

Finally, although I have not attempted to answer the question about why we humans are so fascinated with simulations, I may have provided by the style of analysis undertaken, an indication of how to avoid the worst tendencies to fall into either utopian or dystopian slippery slope positions. Technologies do become embodied, but never totally nor in fully transparent ways. That is how they give us the powers and possibilities we would not otherwise have. But the price of this power entails a subtle and graded sense that while we use and even partially embody our technologies, we also ultimately remain the contingent humans we are. The very ability to step into a multiplicity of our technologies—and thus to also step out of them—is the existential indicator of this constraint for even the best simulation. It is also the point that calls for our constant need for critique.

12

Multistability and Cyberspace

During the early days of radio broadcasting, Georg von Bekesy, later to win a Nobel Prize for his work on sensory inhibition, made an interesting discovery of an auditory-perceptual *multistability*. Radio listeners, listening to music from crystal radios with headphones, sometimes found the music appearing to come from behind their heads, sometimes from before their heads, and sometimes in the middle of their heads. I shall not here follow the complex physical-physiological analysis undertaken by Bekesy, which involves a 180 degree forward/backward projection as well as a centered one, but only note that he was able to teach the listeners to "fix" the music into any one of the preferred positions.

I use the term *multistability* to refer to perceptual variations that exceed the usually noted bivariational ambiguities, such as Wittgensteinian "duck-rabbits," "face-vase" alternations, and the like. For my purposes today I shall largely deal with tristable illustrations, which parallel my earlier example worked out on page 47.

Pardon me if I here repeat the variations again: This illustration is usually taken as a bi-stable one in which one possible variation is to see it as a stage. In this case the central platform is the floor upon which the actors take their places and the three backdrops are the usually painted backdrops for the stage itself. In this variation the top backdrop is to the rear and thus the whole configuration is a 3-D one and the observer sees it as if seated in a balcony looking into and onto the stage. A second reversed variation is possible: in this case we might have a Mayan pyramid and we might be flying over it in a helicopter. Now what was previously the stage floor becomes the top platform of the pyramid and the other three sides are sloping downward from this elevated platform—a reversal of the 3-D effect of the first variation.

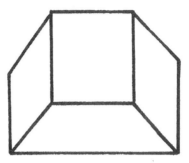

Figure 12.1. Multistable Figure.

But a third variation is also possible: in this case we see a "headless robot" coming toward us: the upper square is his body; the bottom line the ground upon which he is walking; and the side lines are crutches for his arms and legs, which are the remaining lines out from his central body. He then becomes a 2-D variation upon the drawing, thus *tristability*.

It is usually claimed that William Gibson coined the term *cyberspace* in his fictional book *The Neuromancer*, and certainly it is from this source that so much hype and conversation has occurred concerning cyberphenomena, to which one can add the term, coined by Jaron Lanier, *virtual reality*. What I propose to do here is to apply a limited *phenomenology* to these phenomena which I shall call *cyberspace multistabilities*. I begin by applying tristability to a video display screen.

I begin with screen space. First, screen space presents the possibility of at least a limited range of perceptual, spatial variations. The first may be called, on-the-screen space. Here, the example most clearly associates with the *textual* as in word processing, reading Internet matter, or e-mail text. The written words appear on the screen and usually there is lacking either "depth" or distance projection. If one is careful, of course, one notes that this form of "flat" screen space is actually quite different from its analogues on paper or in books. The former is backlighted via either the usual video display device or an LED screen. The backlighting retains opacity, and in the earlier word processing screens, lettering was green, later amber, before becoming multi-colored and accommodating images more contemporarily. But for less than critical perception, the on-the-screen spatiality is basically "flat" and without depth. (For reference purposes here, it corresponds to the "headless robot" or 2-D variation of my multistable illustration.)

A second variation might be called through-the-screen space, and locates in a virtual spatiality "beyond" the surface of the screen. Here, the associations are best noted with such phenomena as computer or video game presentations. In those with the best graphics, while the surface of the screen remains as a sort of "echo" presence and can be noted, it remains more a fringe phenomenon by merely framing the video display. The graphic entities locate themselves better in the cyberspace of near-distance, beyond or through the screen. In this variation, the projection is enhanced by being audiovisual and the dancing dragons, warriors, or auto thieves play out their roles in the space through-the-screen. Never mind that were these virtual actors in "real" bodily space, they would all be miniature in size and located in a near-space. More of this shortly.

I contend that the "opening" from on-the-screen to its framed, miniatured projection in near-cyberspace through-the-screen, opens what I call a *technological trajectory*. Put most simply, if better "realism" can be attained through the framed and miniaturized near-cyberspace, why not approximate even more to a bodily lifeworld by enhancing it even more? It is here that the trajectory to today's largely hyped and not yet delivered *virtual reality* projections are made. These would be close to being in-the-screen.

Ideally, to attain this trajectory several things would have to happen. First, one would have to move from the reduced sensory dimensions of the visual only, text on-the-screen, through the audiovisual video games through-the-screen, to a much more multidimensional, whole body in-the-screen. One would have to have full sensory dimensions and have the cyberworld "surround" one. The imaginations of such a state range from the movie, *Truman* in which a human finds himself in a fully virtual world, to the still-crude attempts to approximate whole body experience in the body cages that move and the humans who are encapsulated in computerized gloves and goggles, but which cocoons remain "echo" effects that continue to distract from free whole body experience. Or, current technologies take the shape of larger, unframed displays such as IMAX, in which the display reaches to the same parameters as the angles of my visual field. But anything like a fully in-the-screen experience remains at present limited and rather primitive.

To this point I have been emphasizing what could be called the screen "world" or that which appears as an electronic "environmental focus." What is experienced "out there" in the range from text to an audio-video-kinesthetic "world"? In the previous chapter, I moved to the situated bodily coordinate and noted its multistable variations, the POVs. I shall not repeat these here.

The next movement of my analysis takes a look at the structured non-neutrality of cyber and virtual technologies. In this case, rather than the focus upon full sensory experience and motility, I will focus upon expressivity and the way in which affects get shaped. Here, my primary phenomena will be e-mail and the Internet and the recent modifications of social media such as Twitter, Facebook, and related multimedia variants, with the associated communications which these mediate.

I remember well when intra-university e-mail was introduced at Stony Brook. At first, this was a medium that took on the appearance of replacing the flow of paper memoranda with electronic ones. One would have thought e-mail to be an analogue to written communications—but it did not long remain this way (although as a vestigial function memoranda and news still get distributed). Instead, e-mail quickly took the shape of what I called the "party line" telephone. I have in mind the old farm telephone systems in which an entire neighborhood was on the same line. From dean's memoranda to a version of phone tag about when to meet for lunch was the quick pattern change in the early days.

Here we meet again what I have called an "instrumental inclination," which occurs in the adoption and adaptation of new technologies. Many possibilities are open and none are determinative, but not all get followed and over time a sort of "center of gravity" in uses emerges. At first, the extant uses in previous media simply get transferred to the new medium—official memoranda or textual phone calls. (I want to note that minor cultural differences are sometimes retained, in my experience Americans tend to think of e-mail as more "telephonic" and yield both very quick replies and an informal tone, whereas many of my European friends have indicated they think of it as more like letter correspondence and, with exceptions, tend to be slower in response and somewhat more "formal" in tone.)

Clearly, both the temporal and spatial presentation of electronic communication is different from either writing or telephone. It is "nearer" and faster than writing; but not quite so immediate and demanding of a "real time" presence as the telephone. I find this median space-time to be the primary advantage of e-mail. Assuming a community of users who are regular users, one can expect a relatively fast reply and yet not have to experience the frustrations of "phone tag," as it is commonly called. E-mail, of course, retains the irreal near distance of most mediated communications, in which there is no geographical "near" or "far," but all electronic spaces are roughly equivalent and all display "near-distance." And, insofar as e-mail remains a written "text" it also remains a sensorily reduced medium.

Yet, sensory reduction does not preclude—indeed, I suspect it allows—a weird kind of amplification of the expressive and the affective. Here is one example of this phenomenon: the "LISTSERVE war." In my department there are periodic "LISTSERVE wars," made possible by a combined faculty and graduate student e-mail LISTSERVE. Topics are highly variable—an analytic philosopher named Brian Leiter issues an Internet ranking of philosophy departments. Ranks are measured by his own informed, but idiosyncratic reputational rankings such that if well-known Prof A moves from Department X to Department Y, the ranking of the losing department may well fall. Clearly, this is a piece of information that stimulates lots of controversy. That controversy has periodically erupted in my department, which is dominantly "continental" and thus does not rise to prominence in the Leiter Report. But, of late, particularly since the Leiter Report does not regard Harvard as at the top level, now across the country there is a growing (analytic) resistance to this report and counterlists, rankings, and condemnations are appearing on the Net.

LISTSERVE wars, however, need not be about overtly controversial items—they can be over seeming trivialities. We had one about "cows." It was claimed that most animal names are gendered—cock/hen; buck/doe; stud/bitch; etc. but that in the case of cows, while there was bull/heifer, the term *cow* was generic. ("Cattle" is the actual generic term.) I cannot tell you how long this LISTSERVE war went on, with humor, but often more serious and offended responses. And, there have been other topics as well, but I began to notice that the patterns of the LISTSERVE wars were the same, regardless of topic.

Here, roughly, is what happens: at first a limited number of participants enter the wars, messages might be fairly detailed and sometimes fairly passionate, but as the war continues the messages get shorter, more colloquial, and often more angry. Also, there seems to be a kind of self-selectivity which sets in, the "nitpickers" gradually take over, and then, eventually the topic simply fades away.

Returning to the notion of an "instrumental inclination," which is not a determination, my suspicion is that the relatively easy and quick form of communication, in this case to a wider set of participants than even a "party line," inclines toward a high lack of reflectivity. E-mail allows the dashing-off of what first comes to mind. One rarely edits and the Send button is too easily available.

A second aspect of this instrumental inclination is an equal sense of presumed intimacy. E-mail comes from many, many sources and, at least in my experience, it often is quickly "intimate," sometimes simply in the use of first names, equally in the use of highly informal and even abbreviated language, and sometimes it rises to the presumptive. It is very rare for me these days to get an e-mail addressed: Herr Professor Doctor Ihde! Extreme cases of e-mail intimacy have been publicized with respect to e-mail romances, many of which have highly comic results, such as the fat man in bright pink pants

who showed up for an entire weekend on an island at the invitation of his
female inviter, and some have tragic results, such as first date rapes and in a
few cases, murders.

One must be careful here. For example, it is quite likely that distance
matches, for example among the nineteenth-century mail-order brides, could
always carry this danger. But with electronic communication there has emerged
the notion of an "avatar." Reduced sensory presentation carries the possibility of magnified nonpresence. Electronic communications, for instance with
teleconferencing, allow for audiovisual, real time over distance communication.
We use it for our doctoral dissertation exams in the German-American *Col-
legium Transatanticum Philosophae*. The American faculty in the United States
teleconference with their German counterparts over telephone-computer video
and the candidate, located at one university, responds to questioners from both.

One technology projected some decades ago—the audiovisual telephone—
at first did not catch on. Philip Brey, in analyzing this problem, noted that
many users were fearful that were they to be projected in their actual setting,
they might be caught in embarrassing situations. The Philips Company then
experimented with the development of avatars that could be projected instead.
Later, of course, the multiuse cell phone did catch on and includes camera
and projection functions. And with it, parallel with Internet social media,
there has been a groundswell of changed cultural practices, often overtly
exhibitionistic and voyeuristic. These have taken both textual (Twitter) and
imagistic forms (Facebook), with uncontrolled distribution possibilities. Note,
however, that this distribution and immediacy potential already lurked in the
previous technologies noted above. As the technologies, particularly the social
media, catch on there is also a change in cultures: what earlier was more
self-conscious, now moves toward more self-display or even exhibitionism.

The third dimension of space-time transformation I wish to investigate
here related to the phenomena of virtual/actual alternation. I begin quite
concretely with contemporary academic conferences. I myself often learn of
conferences through the Internet, via e-mail. My inviter may well be someone
I have never met in person, but who introduces himself or herself through an
e-mail. If agreements are reached and plans are laid for attending, then as with
the conference, travel and lodging arrangements are also made electronically.
All this virtuality, however, leads to an actual occasion, where in face-to-face
meetings previously virtually known persons become personally acquainted.
This alternation is not unusual, but is in fact today's norm for almost all the
"jet-profs" I know. (I even wonder if the very few holdouts from e-mail do
not gradually get shunted aside?) The spatial-temporal transformations here are
alternations, multistabilities. The near space-time of cyberspace alternates with

the temporally shrunken, larger geographical space-time of contemporary travel. But the incommensurability is not a foreground feature of our contemporary life.

Beyond the relative sameness of intercontinental academic life lie the more extreme transformations of what I call "pluriculture." Pluriculture is the mediation of multiple cultures via the virtual space-time of contemporary communications. The evening news is one such mediation: within the space of a few minutes, the cultural presence of Israelis, Afghanistanis, Pakistanis, Chinese, Russians, varieties of Europeans all parade before us on the screen. We become aware of more cultures in a single news broadcast than most Medieval kings knew of in a long reign. But, more. What is displayed virtually over the news, is also alternatively actually displayed in the cosmopolitan centers of today. Every major urban city has a multiplicity of ethnic restaurants, with cuisines reaching far beyond Europe and into the Middle and Far East and probably to Africa. Similarly, in fashion the culture fragments that can be chosen for dress bricolage are also actually available in the markets and stores of cosmopolitan centers.

Two extremes may be found within this virtual/actual pluriculture: on the one hand, there is a growing, multicultural cosmopolitanism. The gradual increase of world travelers often brings a kind of sophistication and adaptability that promotes an ease with multiple or multistable practices. The switch from forks and knives in European restaurants to chopsticks in Asian ones is made without effort. But at the other extreme there lie the movements to ethnic purification and hegemony which mark almost all the major controversies of today's interconnected virtual/actual world. The embrace of the cosmopolitan is countered by the reaction to the multicultural. Yet both trajectories are mediated by the cyber-technologies of today. But not equally. Clearly, interconnection is unevenly distributed, with the so-called first world highly interconnected. Yet, even the most isolated areas of the world are interconnected with cell phones. And there are surprises—for example, although illegal and discouraged, in my visit to Iran some years ago, it was obvious that at least urban people are interconnected. The rooftops have gardens of satellite dishes and my invitation there had developed in exactly the same virtual/actual alternations as other locations. The time of my visit was just after the ban on supporting Iranian graduate students was lifted and I found myself entertained by a group of university students wanting to know about American graduate education. Similarly, a neighboring country, Pakistan, sends inquiries for graduate school to my now outdated director's address with such profusion that I sometimes wonder if everyone wants to come to an American graduate school. I do not have the data, but it would be interesting to see how a plotting of Internet connections and distributions maps upon or not upon the regions of highest ethnic diversity versus ethnic withdrawal. All this, however, is anecdotal and impressionistic.

Prognostic Conclusion

I have undertaken a very short, mostly phenomenological look at some aspects of multistability in cyberspace and in virtual/actual alternations. This work has been descriptive, not normative, and not yet prognostic in character. I should like to conclude with a few passing speculations based upon patterns that have emerged from many technological trajectories. Doing this is always risky business, particularly if one keeps even recent prognoses in mind: Edward Tenner lists some of these in his *Why Things Bite Back,* such as Toffler's prediction that the coming of the electronic era would produce the "paperless society," or the prediction by an early computer executive that all foreseeable data could be handled by a single, large computer with a few gigabytes of capacity.

First some fears: As the Internet grows and grows, even if loose-linked, the capacity of overload also increases. I find myself fighting mightily to keep out "Spam" and the growth of intrusive advertising and commercialization. I suspect this is a losing battle and the American television model of ads taking up virtually as much time as the movie may well prevail. Secondly, again because of networking and loose-linking, I doubt that either "democratization" or "centralization" models will apply to an interlinked world. Rather, a noise model will likely apply in which cacophony is the dominant feature as all the voices are raised. This simply places us in the position we already know partially with information overload, which, in turn, calls for ever more critical hermeneutic processes to weed through that information. Third, continued deformation of the private/public distinction seems likely to occur. Electronic information seems both quasi-eternal (think of all the e-mails retrieved in criminal cases or with respect even to presidents) and yet evanescent (obsolescence of technologies removes more information from recovery than ever imagined, or larger crashes and systems deletions or magnetic deterioration move in directions opposite stability.)

But these are not very interesting prognoses. More interesting are those which point to changes in the very style and substance of communication. Here, it is our younger users who probably show the direction. Remotes, controlling ever larger numbers of channels, seem simply to lead to smaller and smaller fragments of meaning. The nanosecond switches are reminiscent of the dominant style of MTV with rapid image-switches, or, alternatively, of the multiscreen presences and switches seen in newsroom control panels, or, the latest from my son's world, instant messaging, which seems to have a three-word maximum phrase for a sentence. Who can read more than a few pages by scrolling? Who can "listen" if the message exchanges are too long?

Yet, while this may be the center of gravity or inclination of direction in most electronic media, they do not stand alone, nor are they the only alternatives. The papered society is still healthy, with more books being published than ever before, and what was on the scroll can be printed out. Just as the virtual/actual alternation occurs contemporarily, so does the instant/durational alternation of multiple instantiations of information. Yet, overall, more speed and more quantity does seem presently triumphant. Cyberspace—and cyber-time—displays both a multistability and yet also a "closer-quicker" space-time.

13

Variations on the *Camera Obscura*

Isomorphic Cameras

During the spring semester of my first year at Stony Brook University, I had my first experience of a *camera obscura*. On March 7, 1970, there was to be a full solar eclipse which would be 74 percent visible on Long Island. The newspapers announcing this event cautioned that one must avoid direct eyeball observation of the sun's occlusion, and suggested the construction of a "pinhole camera," with directions included in the articles. So, by taking a cardboard box, cutting a small opening on one side and pasting aluminum foil with a very small pinhole over the opening, then pasting a white sheet of paper on the inside of the box, on the opposite side, one could take the box out and the image of the sun as it underwent gradual occlusion appeared on the white paper "screen" pasted on the side opposite the aperture. Thus, I and my family could now safely watch the progression of the eclipse as the moon gradually occluded the disc of the sun.

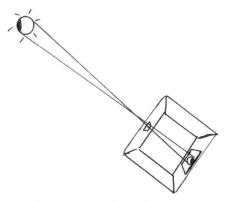

Figure 13.1. Cardboard Box Pinhole Camera.

155

We were, on that occasion, repeating a very ancient practice of eclipse observation, which may have been the first scientific or astronomical optical experiment to which the *camera obscura* was put. Indeed, the first such described use in the context of a treatise on optics was that of Al Hazen, the Arab natural philosopher, in 1037. Vitello and Roger Bacon picked up on the camera and its optics in Europe by 1270. But, historically, knowledge of the *camera* is more ancient that that. The Chinese mathematician, Mo Ti, described this device with its inverted image in the fifth century BCE, calling it "the locked treasure room." Aristotle and Euclid in Hellenic times, fourth century BCE, also knew the optic effect. The camera really picked up European interest during the Renaissance, a time when many practices were being technologized. For example, the dominant and sacred music, usually vocal, was experiencing a proliferation of new instruments, including most of the strings, woodwinds, brass, and percussion instruments. In visual art the camera began to play its role, along with many other technologies used to measure and fix precise "Renaissance perspective" preferences.

Alberti used a large dark room camera to create highly verisimilitudinous paintings as early as 1437; Leonardo da Vinci described his own use of the camera to image and draw a crucifix in 1450. In 2001, David Hockney, apparently thinking he had rediscovered this practice, published *Secret Knowledge: Rediscovering the Lost Techniques of the Old Masters* (Penguin Putnam, 2001), in which he asserted that many of the Renaissance masters had used the camera. The book was introduced to an overflow audience at New York University and met with outrage from many art critics at what appeared to them to be a form of "cheating" to produce art with the aid of technological instruments. Many of us, more familiar with the histories of science and technology, were amused—including Catherine Wilson, the historian of microscopy, and myself— since this history had long been known and documented, for instance in my favorite 1929 *Encyclopedia Britannica* (the same set that contains Husserl's first entry on "phenomenology"). During Renaissance times such instruments were thought to be highly useful since Giovanni Battista Della Porta recommended them for making pictures in a 1558 treatise.

It may be interesting to note at this point, that Renaissance art practice apparently preceded use of the camera in science, although it did receive its name (*camera obscura*) from Johannes Kepler, who used it for astronomical and surveying purposes in the seventeenth century. Galileo used a version of the camera known as a helioscope to observe sunspots in 1610. Let us now look at the instrument itself in its early forms, consider its elements, and then follow some of its variations, which have resulted in multiple trajectories of use.

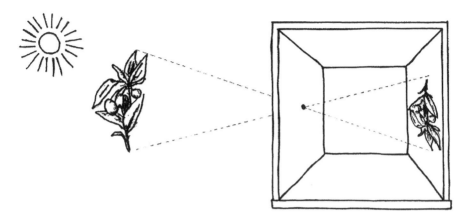

Figure 13.2. Isomorphic Camera Obscura.

The ancient camera was a simple device, and here I want to define its elements as (1) a light source, often simply the sun or outdoor daylight; (2) an aperture or opening that, in effect, "squeezes" the light that enters the dark room; whereupon the incoming light then casts an image upon (3) a light-colored, preferably white, screen opposite. As in the illustrations, then, some outside object—or the light source itself, for example, the sun as in eclipse—casts its image onto the screen. I am now going to take this optical process and show how, *through multiple variations,* the camera ends up producing a whole series of multistable phenomena, which serve as an equally multiple set of results in artistic, scientific, entertainment, and other contexts.

In the "Alberti" variant, the artist can step inside the dark room and see the colored, moving image of the tree, which is located outside the room, illuminated by the sun. A first-time experience can here be an "aha" one, since one is surprised by the verisimilitude of the depiction. What often stands out at first is the *isomorphism* of the image—it is "just like the outside scene!"—which later would be repeated photographically. But, a more critical look shows *that the image is not fully isomorphic, it is also transformed.* The most obvious transformation is that the image is upside down (inverted). Secondly, the image is reduced in size. Thirdly, the image is less vivid and sometimes less clear and distinct than the scene imaged. Finally, the camera transforms the scene in two additional ways which relate specifically to the style of much Renaissance painting: it automatically reduces three dimensions to two on the screen; and it produces a "Renaissance perspective" realism (without mathematics). To further illustrate optical transformations, I will skip to a relatively recent camera experience of my own with the very large camera that today operates as a tourist attraction in Edinburgh, Scotland.

This camera is located in a turret and includes a set of mirrors, such that when the complex aperture is moved, the image can vary. The image is cast upon a very large parabolic surface, to lessen the spatial distortions that at this size would occur on a flat screen. Thus, what one sees inside the viewing space is a quite "realistic" depiction of the cityscape or active street scenes outside. The guide then plays a cute trick: she takes a white card and extends it over the surface, and whatever is being imaged—cars, people walking, trams—suddenly appear on the card. By lifting or lowering the card it appears that one is now lifting or lowering the objects depicted. This entertainment practice was exploited as early as the eighteenth century, with projection versions of the camera used to produce phantasms and early versions of horror shows. However, the point I want to make here is that the camera in producing its images, transforms, reshapes what is being imaged. Its isomorphism is never pure or total. But, phenomenologically, this is not to be thought of as negative; quite to the contrary, the transformations themselves are precisely what makes for new phenomena, which in the case of scientific practice also produce or stimulate new knowledge.

In the example-set so far discussed, drawn from different historical periods and different stages of the camera's development, one can discern that a richer and more complex trajectory from the ancient camera has taken place. In its earliest form, the camera was a genuine "pinhole camera" with a small, simple, round hole forming the aperture. Probably the earliest "improvement" on the aperture was the addition of some kind of *lens*. A lens, particularly if focusable, could improve the clarity of the image, or, as in Galileo's use of it as a helioscope combined with a telescope, produce an image from an object too far away to show its particularities—in this case, sunspots—without magnification. In the case of the helioscope, the instrument is already *compound*, that is, a telescope has been added to the camera's screen. I shall call these early variations on the camera, here primarily taking note of innovations in the aperture, *high isomorphism* variants. But I shall now speed up both the histories and variations on the camera.

Non-Isomorphic Cameras

Returning to scientific practices concerning the camera, the next major development occurred toward the end of the seventeenth century (experiments 1666, published 1677). Here the inventor was Isaac Newton who—unknowingly—began the development which led to a very different style of camera imaging, which I shall call *non-isomorphic imaging*. Newton, like Galileo before him, was an optics maker and aware that prisms produced rainbow spectra of colors. He reported, "I procured me a triangular glass prism to try therewith the celebrated phenomenon of colors. . . . Having darkened my chamber and made a small hole in my windowshuts to let in a convenient quantity of the sun's light, I placed my prism at its entrance, that it might be thereby refracted to the opposite wall."[1] In short, a *camera obscura*, but this time with a prism instead of either pinhole or lens. In one sense, this is a simple variation upon the aperture; note early that the hole, still round, remains the same. But the prism produces a very different type of image.

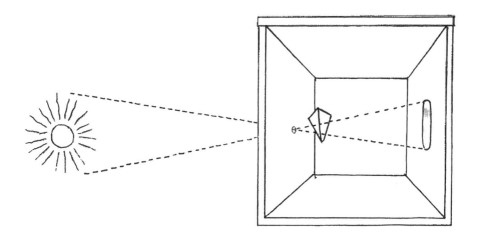

Figure 13.3. Newton's Prism Camera.

What appears on the screen of the opposite wall is a lengthened, rounded oblong of a "rainbow spectrum" with seven multiple colors of that spectrum, but without clear distinctions at the borders of each color. It was from this experiment that Newton derived his theory of colors and recognized that "white" light was, in fact, made up of a range of different colors. Later, brilliantly recognizing that different colors have what today we would call different frequencies, Newton realized that he could avoid a certain limitation found in the refracting telescopes of his time, known as the "chromatic distortion." By using a parabolic mirror, he could refocus all of the distinct frequencies of colors onto one spot and thus increase the magnification power of a new *reflecting telescope*. I will not trace all the other science that arose from this new image production by the camera, but will underline that the new images thus opened the way to the production of new knowledge.

Returning to a phenomenology of the new imaging, we can note that the spectrum, unlike the previous camera transformations of imaged phenomena into produced images, is *not isomorphic* in the sense that the spectrum on the opposite wall is nothing "like" the sun outside that is the light source for the image, either in shape, color, or other ordinary perceptual aspects. While I shall not examine this change here, as I have claimed elsewhere this image is more a "signature" or hermeneutic phenomenon, which has to be "read" to be understood. Newton took this phenomenon to relate to the beam of light itself. The beam, white, was decomposable into its seven constituent colors. The reason for this suggestion will become apparent below. It is, however, a major and different stability than that of isomorphic imaging and a new output for the camera.

While Newton's development the camera, modifying Galileo's isomorphic helioscope to a non-isomorphic proto-spectroscope took fifty years (roughly 1610 to 1666), the next step to a genuine spectroscope took longer. First, in 1802, W. H. Wollaston, followed in 1810 by Joseph Frauenhofer, produced and noted the appearance of *spectral lines*.[2] What produced these distinct lines was yet another variation on the aperture of the camera, by which both Wollaston and Frauenhofer replaced Newton's round hole with a *slit*, which produced through the prism a narrower and more distinct color range, showing only one color. Frauenhofer, now varying what I am calling the light source, also discovered that flame-cast spectra showed discrete bright lines, while sun-cast spectra contained numerous dark lines as well. The first practical astronomical spectrometer, however, did not reach full development until 1859, when the collaboration of G. R. Kirchkoff and R. Bunsen produced multicolored spectra, complete with the bright and dark lines for sun and star spectra. And, they discovered, spectra with individual patterns could be associated with specific elemental chemical signatures. Kirchkoff recognized that the same bright yellow lines from a sodium salt flame casting also appeared in the sun-cast spectrum in its yellow range. (This yellow range had been recognized earlier by Frauenhofer, who dubbed it "D lines.") Kirchkoff recognized that the sun must also have sodium as one of its chemical elements, and thus, beyond Newton, that sunlight was light produced by a chemical constituent. In short, the full hermeneutic signature had been recognized, and, with the proper hard work associated with this new science, *spectra could be read*.[3] There followed in astronomy the first development of star classification by chemical composition.

Isomorphic and Non-Isomorphic Variations

My narrative has drawn from the messy, sporadic history of producing new optical versions of the camera, which at this point discloses two trajectories: an isomorphic trajectory, in which the images produced can be perceptually recognized as having degrees of similarity between the object and its image (despite the transformation differences also shown); and the non-isomorphic, which produces a "readable" image that does not resemble the object imaged. I now turn to more variations on the camera, taking one example from each trajectory.

In the case of the isomorphic trajectory, it will come as no surprise that the *photographic camera* fits into the ancient *obscura* versions' history. The famous Eastman Kodak camera is a hand-held, miniaturized version of the *camera obscura,* albeit with differences. In this case, the aperture is fitted with a lens—to which has been added at least a shutter (to control the exposure time of the light source) and, in more complex technologies, a focusing device. Yet the simple elements of the ancient camera remain. Photographic cameras vary the *screen,* so that instead of the *tabula rasa* blank wall, a plate with image-fixing chemistry has been substituted, in early cameras a chemical-coated plate, in later ones a chemically sensitive film. The desire to fix the image, with experiments to find the proper fixing agent, dates from the eighteenth century, but for practical purposes the process, invented by Joseph Niepce and purchased by Louis Daguerre, took useable shape in 1839, followed by a rapid explosion of photography immediately thereafter.

This variant on the camera returns us to a dramatic image isomorphism. The earliest photographs were striking in their "realism," and the move to photo portraiture produced much commentary, including some bemoaning the likely death of painted portraiture, and some commenting on the "living death" appearance of the still image, preservable for eons. The scientific adaptation of photography was virtually immediate, with the first telescope-aided photo of the gibbous moon in 1840.[4]

The non-isomorphic trajectory was also developing more variants during the prolific nineteenth century. Thomas Young, in 1803, developed what today is called the "double slit" experiment, yet another version of the aperture variation of the camera. In this case, the light source, now split by several techniques into a double projection, shows the "interference" of two wave patterns.

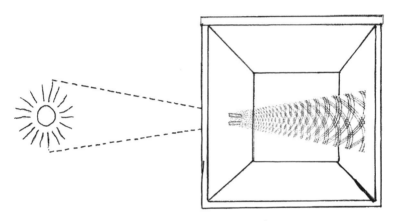

Figure 13.4. Young's Twin Slit Camera.

Today, this variant has led to *interferometry*, which reappears anew in quantum imaging. Double slit versions of the camera produce the patterns of wave/particle images and quantum entanglement, which draws so much attention. In its own day, it was a powerful demonstration of *wave phenomena*, which Young was convinced was characteristic of light itself.

Phenomenologically, if one slit yields new image phenomena that fit into the ultimate history of chemical signatures, and two slits yield depictions of wave phenomena, might not one wonder what *multiple slits* might yield? Now, while I have found no evidence that such tinkering or playfulness occurred with this suggestion, it is the case that the use of multiple slits—in this case *diffraction gratings*—did play a significant role in spectroscopic development.

And although some historians credit multiple-slit devices to David Rittenhouse as early as 1785, Frauenhofer, with his interest in the yellow D spectrum, did construct a useable diffraction grating (1821). This was a device that, in effect, created many slits with wires closely spaced in parallel through which the light source could be cast. These multiple slit devices became quite standard in many spectroscopic practices.

To this point, I have highlighted some of the variants within a twenty-four-century history (2400 BP to 110 BP) of the camera. I have noted two major trajectories: the isomorphic trajectory in which the image phenomenon produced is easily perceptually recognized as appearing to be "like" whatever object is being imaged; and a non-isomorphic trajectory in which the image phenomenon does not appear to be perceptually "like" what is being imaged, but rather is some kind of signature that can be "read." The difference between the two trajectories is produced by varying some aspect of the camera's technology. In my examples to this point, variations of the aperture (simple hole, lens, prism, slit, double, and multiple slits) change the image-phenomenon. Less prominent are variations upon the screen (blank opaque screen or photographic plate/film) and the light source (sunlight, flame, or artificial light).

I contend that in the twentieth and twenty-first centuries one finds a much more complex, and also much accelerated set of developments, within which one can still recognize variations upon the camera and its optics. But in this case, much of the innovation arises from late modern—and postmodern—capacities to alter the light source. The light source analogue also becomes "active" in the sense that what is beamed is constructed or manipulated. Granted, the decomposition of "white" light into its constituent colors, as in spectroscopy, already does this, but in a limited way. For example, Newton argued that seven and only seven colors constituted the composition of "white" light or what we regard today as the optical range of light. He was unaware of the range of infrared and ultraviolet wavelengths, which, while still optical, lie beyond the horizons of human perception. Many of our near-cousins within the animal kingdom would be surprised at this ignorance!

Postmodern and Posthuman Imaging

I now return to the simpler narrative style being followed here. What begins to happen in the twentieth century, in the context of the history of the camera, is that new ability to manipulate the camera's light source becomes available. Indeed, at the very end of the nineteenth century, the discovery by W. C. Roentgen of X-rays (1895) and the subsequent use of X-ray cameras was a major breakthrough for camera variations. Here, the light source, X-radiation, could now penetrate through many types of material objects—in Roentgen's early work, human flesh—and image only more dense material. Roentgen took an X-ray image of his wife's hand that showed her bone structure and ring, which he published and sent copies of to many people, and as with the rapid spread of photography, soon many people were building versions of the X-ray camera. The radiation here, of course, was not optical—it was *beyond* the optical.

In the context of the camera, we now have a radically transformed light source, which now produces a new image phenomenon. In one sense it retains a certain isomorphism (the bones of Roentgen's wife can easily be recognized as those of a human hand), but now it is a strange kind of isomorphism since no ordinary visual experience gives the sort of "seeing through" that the X-ray image shows. One must, I hold, do some *translating* to comprehend this newly depicted phenomenon. In the early days of X-ray use, imaging of injuries, such as gunshot wounds, was an almost immediate application. In this case, the perceptual isomorphism remained relatively simple—anyone could recognize the location of the bullet in a skull, for example. Yet, it was an interior visual display not possible from any external observation of a bullet hole on the surface of a skull. It was an *extension* of vision, but one that produced what could not be directly perceived.

The twentieth century opened a plethora of what I have above called light-source variations. Remaining within the context of the camera, light-source manipulability included the use of electrons, ions, photons, and, from the mid-twentieth century, coherent light, as with lasers. Equally, the proliferation of instrumental imaging technologies is simply too large and complex to follow fully here. For example, mass spectroscopy, which often uses ion beams for its active light source, can identify in the usual hermeneutic fashion noted above with optical spectroscopy, the chemical signatures of very specific items. For example, obsidian, which is a volcanic by-product, can be identified with the specific volcano that produces it. It was through this process that anthropologists interested in human migration discovered that obsidian artifacts deposited on a Pacific Island some three thousand miles from their volcanic source served as evidence of ancient sea voyages by Pacific Island peoples. Similarly, the specific signatures of mass spectroscopic analysis of the famous Otzi's (the 5300 BP Ice Age Man discovered in the Italian Alps in 1991) stomach contents were able to identify red deer and mountain sheep as part of his last meal when alive. These examples remain primarily upon the non-isomorphic trajectory side.

Contemporarily on the isomorphic trajectory, one also finds *holography*. Invented by Dennis Gabor in 1947, at first this unique 3-D technique remained difficult to produce. As a variant upon electron microscopy, electron beams were used at first, but with the introduction of the coherent light of the laser (1960) practical holography could develop. Transmission holography, by which laser light is cast through the compounded film to produce the image on the side opposite the light source, entails a sort of backward camera. In the physics building of my university there is a display of "kiss II" (1974). At its core is a composed "photo-hologram" consisting of 360 frames from a motion picture, lighted from below, casts an image (in 3-D) of a young woman who raises her hand, winks, and throws a kiss as the viewer walks by.

Before leaving my contemporary examples, I want to mention one more *beam active* variant on the camera. This variant, described in *Scientific American*, consists of a laser pointer (coherent light) whose beam is cast through a diffraction grating with the screen image phenomenon showing the resultant photon spin (there are four possible spin vectors).

As noted, the possibilities of manipulated active beams has opened, largely in the late-twentieth and into the twenty-first century, a whole new series of camera variants. But we may now summarize and condense the history of the camera(s), to take note of the patterns that have emerged over the twenty-six centuries' existence of these imaging devices.

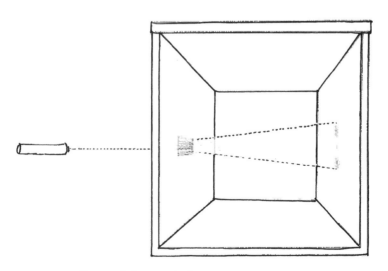

Figure 13.5. Laser-Diffraction Grate Camera.

Variations and Multistabilities

In this concluding section, I must begin with a context and some disclaimers: This chapter is, in effect, a condensation of some of my now decade and a half of research into *imaging technologies*. The manuscript for a potential book is now more than three hundred pages long, tentatively titled *Imaging Technologies: Plato upside Down*. It is both a history and phenomenology of these technologies and the discovery that *variations upon the camera obscura*—seven or eight—which account for the dominant forms of much science imaging, emerged slowly. In part, that is what I have condensed here. In this research, both reflecting my own interests but also reflecting a need to keep the project within manageable size, I focus upon scientific use of imaging technologies. But there are equal or even greater uses of these technologies in art (noted in part here), in entertainment (more often in modernity related to projective imaging such as cinema, television, and video screens, examples that I did not pursue in this chapter), and even warfare (simulation and long-range robotics as examples). This research shaped my first deep history set of examinations of technologically multistable developments. The next chapter will take up an even deeper history, that of the bow-under-tension.

First, a summary of a phenomenologically oriented history of the camera; (1) I have analyzed the camera into a minimum of constituent elements: light source, aperture, room or camera size, screen for displaying the image-phenomenon; (2) I have contended that in its now twenty-five-plus-centuries history, the camera has undergone a development through variations upon elements or parts, each of which produces transformations in its output or resultant image-phenomenon; and (3) whatever human praxis—art, science, entertainment—has used this technology, has equally transformed its results. In the case of science, here focal, the result has been some newly produced knowledge which can be discovered, produced, or constructed in relation to the camera and its image-phenomenon.

Here follows a schematic set of aspects relating to the camera:

Light source	Aperture	Camera	Screen

From Mo Ti, in 450 BCE (2460 BP), to roughly 1500 CE (1511 BP), the camera uses ambient light (sun), a small, round hole aperture, with usually room or camera size big enough to accommodate observers. The image-phenomenon, transformed as noted above (inverted, 2-D, isomorphic, etc.) appears on the screen. The experience of the camera could have included the "aha" response to the apparent realism of the scene, but also in some contexts was experienced as something occult and frightening since its inversion was sometimes difficult to accept. What this period shows is that the first developmental *trajectory* of the ancient camera, was *isomorphic,* or "realistic" (as in verisimilitude). Apart from satisfying curiosity (entertainment) interests, by 1037 (Al Hazen) and, later, 1270 (Bacon and Vitello), the camera was being used for scientific observations, particularly eclipses. Al Hazen noted, "The image of the sun at the time of the eclipse, unless it is total, demonstrates that when its light passes through a narrow, round hole and is cast on a plane opposite to he hole it takes on the form of a moon-sickle."[5] As noted above, the camera was a very popular during the Renaissance. Several variations were introduced, for example, although it is not sure who first placed a lens into the aperture, by 1500 CE, Daniel Barbaro claimed that he used lenses.[6] We have already noted the later use of the telescope by Galileo for his helioscope. For art practice, many of the cameras were large enough to accommodate the painter inside. The image-phenomena produced remained isomorphic.

Later, once early modern science was off and running, another aperture variation was introduced by Newton: a prism, which produced a very different image-phenomenon, the seven-color spectrum. Now, unlike the isomorphic trajectory, a non-isomorphic or non-verisimilitudinous imaging was used. In Newton's case the scientific discoveries included (1) his theory of colors and (2) the recognition that light decomposition included recomposition, with the resultant knowledge that different frequencies of light could be refocused for better, reflecting telescopes.

By the nineteenth century, which I will call the beginning age of late modern science, there began to be an accelerated set of experiments upon cameras. Three variations upon the aperture took place. Between 1802 and 1810 the aperture opening became a slit (plus prism), thus producing at will single frequencies or colors of light that displayed interesting bright lines within the color displayed. Wollaston and Frauenhofer were the innovators here, and they remained within the non-isomorphic trajectory. In a parallel development, in 1803–04 Young invented the double slit aperture, which produced wave interference patterns in the image-phenomenon. And not long afterward, in 1821, Frauenhofer constructed the first diffraction grating (multiple slits, in effect). Similarly, light-source variants, which now included sun, flame, and, later, incandescent light were used. As noted above, this experimentation yielded a readable signature from spectra which indicated chemical composition in the light source (sun and stars early, many other materials later).

By 1839, with Daguerre, photographic imaging became practical, following which there occurred one of the most explosive and rapid disseminations of an imaging technology ever. Art, entertainment, history, and science immediately began to use Daguerre's version of the camera. Images proliferated, from family albums to Civil War documentation. As noted above, most early uses of photography were strongly isomorphic, although new knowledge production became possible with refinements in the photographic process. Eduard Muybridge's time-stop photography began to image phenomena hitherto unknown—horses' feet off the ground and human motion studies—and ever-faster time stopping continued. I have not followed this trajectory to motion pictures, but one can see that those, too, are photographic developments.

By the end of the nineteenth century, X-rays became even more powerful beam-active sources for a different kind of visual experience entirely, the visualization of interior structures in terms of their relative density. Nineteenth-century variations also began to show a more inventive, more deliberate tinkering. Additionally, as suggested above, the image-phenomenon of the X-ray depicts what cannot be observed with ordinary perception, and while its isomorphism remains in some sense obvious, it is a deeply transformed isomorphism. This new trajectory opens into the twentieth century.

Constructed Imaging

While I shall open the door to the revolution in imaging that has occurred in the twentieth and twenty-first centuries, I shall not examine it in detail. One of its characteristics is the same as that which emerged with X-rays, the production of images that could depict whole ranges of phenomena lying beyond ordinary, bodily perceptual horizons. Scientifically speaking, today we would talk of the *electro-magnetic spectrum,* which is a wave continuum that spans radiation from the nano-microscopic waves of *gamma* radiation to the kilometer-long waves of *radio emissions.* Not until the twentieth century were there instruments capable of imaging these phenomena. We can perhaps apprehend this by recalling the limitations of Newton's spectrum, which remained limited to our optical, perceptual range of vision. He was unaware of infrared and ultraviolet optical radiation beyond these limits. In contrast, today's astronomy has imaging technologies that can image from gamma to radio waves (Chandra X-ray source, radio astronomy, both infared and ultraviolet telescopes, etc.)

I shall contend that while these instruments remain progeny of the camera, they are less and less like the camera and instead are compounded with another set of technologies, which relate to computerization, computational, digital, and tomographic processes that *construct and manipulate* what becomes the image-phenomenon of this new *constructed imaging.* This is a new trajectory, one in which the instrumentation is actively interventional. Take one example of the new capacities: in most of the science research today (1) practitioners engage a range of different imaging technologies. In medical imaging, for example, CT scans, PET scans MRI and fMRI scans, ordinary X-rays, etc. Each depicts—utilizing different processes—a different "slice" of the object being imaged (say, a brain tumor). But the image-phenomenon produced is also the result of computer processes, which (2) can produce images from data (or data from images in a reversibility), can produce only the slice depiction, or by using tomographic processes, produce a composite. I call these *instrumental phenomenological variations*.

In another context—dating ancient material, for example—one considers a result robust only if several different styles of instrument-embodied measurement have been used (Carbon 14, thermoluminescence, etc.). I shall not here pursue this farther since these processes move in ever more complicated ways in styles no longer like the ancestor cameras.

Within the limits of the already-long history of the camera, I conclude that the multiple trajectories comprised of different styles of imaging, the multiple variations upon the camera machinery, which produce often radically different image-phenomena, and the often gradual perfecting of interpretive insights (a visual hermeneutic) bespeak *multistability* in this material history of instruments related to human practices. The camera has given us vast classes, from photography to holography; it has spawned spectroscopy and interferometry, each with hundreds of types of instruments; and in postmodern guise, it is now linked to digital and computer technologies, instrumental progeny merely mentioned above. In this particular study I have combined histories with phenomenology. With histories, I have noted the long, and often slow use of variations upon some dimension of the camera, with the often innovative new directions in production that followed. With phenomenology, I have stressed *variations* upon the small number of camera elements, each of which produce different and often innovative results. I close with a question: What if a phenomenological inventor began to explore deliberate variations, playfully engaging each to see what resulted? This would be an *experimental technological or material playfulness*. What would happen to the subsequent histories?

14

The Seventh Machine

Bow-under-Tension

This chapter will follow the pattern of the preceding one on the *camera obscura* in the sense that it will draw both from histories and a variational phenomenology of the multiple technologies involved. Indeed, this second phenomenological history is deeper and more multicultural than that of the camera. But in this case I will emphasize a greater contrast between phenomenologically experienceable discoveries and the long histories to which they belong. I begin with what for me was an important "aha" event in my own life.

Musical Improvisation

Many years ago, I was invited to give a keynote presentation at a conference on musical improvisation at the University of California, San Diego. As it turned out, only one other philosopher, Daniel Charles of the University of Paris, was on the program and I knew no one else there. One of the features of this conference was "Improvisation Workshops," which sounded interesting, so, wanting to watch and listen, I picked one and tried to sit off to the side. The studio was filled with different instruments, piano, violins, horns, and also some weird-looking and unrecognizable instruments. And, no, I could not be a mere observer; this was to be an "everyone participates" event. No sooner was I seated than one of the leaders came over and handed me a "water horn." It was an aluminum flat-bottomed flask to which—around the perimeter—brass rods of different lengths had been brazed. It was half-full of water and I was given a violin bow and simply instructed to "play!"

At first, slowly, different participants began to perform—but I quickly discovered nothing was to be orthodox or familiar. The piano players opened the top of the piano and began to bang on the strings with hammers or other pounding devices; the violists, instead of using bows, rubbed their strings with yet other devices; and so in the spirit of improvisation as being defined in action, I picked up my water horn. I sloshed the water around, bowed the brass rods, and then turned it into a percussion device and pounded it on the bench; I even blew across the opening, turning the instrument into a waterwind. One can only imagine the cacophony of this improvised performance—and we learned that it had all had been tape-recorded for posterity (although I never heard the result). This was to become, for me, one of the most dramatic occasions to inform my subsequent understanding of human-technology relations!

If I were to look back, drawing from many, many subsequently published articles, I could easily find premonitions in this event to what became claims concerning human-technology relations:

Clearly, the improvisational use of the instruments violated any "designer intent" regarding designed use;

The uses of even any one instrument were multiple, some totally unplanned and thus, as in so many histories of technologies, could take wildly different trajectories;

Improvisation was a form of deliberate *play*, play—as in imaginative variations—is an essential dimension of phenomenological practice—and for much technological invention;

Improvisation is *overdeterminate* and thus predictabilities become difficult, perhaps impossible;

Each variation suggests or opens up new avenues of development from which new direction can be followed by modifying the original technologies;

The instruments are material devices that engage types of human *embodiment*, bodily actions, to produce the music phenomenon, but also *imagination* is engaged in such a way that the questions are not: *What is this instrument for? What is it? What is its design?* Rather, the questions become: *What can this thing be? What is the range of its possibilities? How far can we go with this?*

While it is possible to see each of the above points relating to the improvisational event, I want now to turn to my second *deep history/phenomenological variations* analysis.

The Seventh Machine

Postmodernity includes the death or the abandonment of *master narratives,* claimed F. Lyotard in his *The Postmodern Condition* (1979), including that of the Western master narrative. This narrative had included the notion that civilization began with Mesopotamia and Egypt; passed on to Greece and Rome; and then Europe and the New World. The origin stories thus always fell into this narrative framework as well. One element of this narrative includes ancient technologies, the *simple machines.* For the Greeks these included the lever, wheel and axle, pulley, wedge, and screw. These were noted by Archimedes during the Hellenic period, in the third century BC (2400 BP). He and later early "technoscientists" (e.g., Heron of Alexandria, 2100 BP) discovered the principles of mechanical advantage and applied these to the simple machines. Later, during a later second major period of this master narrative, the Renaissance, the *inclined plane* was added, making for what became the canonical list of *six simple machines.* These are still taught in elementary school science classes.

This chapter will focus upon a *seventh simple machine,* the bow-under-tension. This "machine," already familiar in Greek and Renaissance times, was also familiar to the much older Egyptian, Mesopotamian, Chinese, Indian, African, and archaic American societies. And, as we shall see, the bow-under-tension goes back at least as far as the Ice Age. In fact, with a few exceptions, the bow-under-tension had been invented and used in almost all cultures. The technology and praxis of *archery* are its most common example.

How old is this technology? If we take archery as its earliest exemplar, it appears that the *arrow* may be its oldest element. Arrow points have been found in Africa dating back as far as 50,000 BP. But—here is the ambiguity— these "arrow points" may have been fixed to quite long shafts, spear length, fitted with fletches, and propelled by spear throwers (as simple machines, throwing levers, as it were). This projectile technology spanned the earth, from woomeras in Australia to atlatls in Meso-America. When the transition occurred to bows-under-tension, instead of spear throwers, to make bows and arrows, remains unknown. But the bow-under-tension was invented almost everywhere (Australia is one exception: the move from woomera to a flying projectile took the form of the boomerang instead). The main difference between an atlatl spear and an arrow would be the length of the arrow, but given that reeds, bamboo, shaped wood, all deteriorate before the stone point, the physical record is poor. However, very early atlatl shafts have been found, complete with *fletching* (the feather guide of an arrow) dating from the period between 27,000 and 20,000 BP. Shorter shafts, more likely to be arrows, go back at least 15,000 BP and probably farther. Here, then, is an extremely ancient simple machine: bow-under-tension used in archery.

This form of the narrative, in several important ways, *does not fit the Western master narrative*: First, the histories relating to the bow-under-tension pre-date by far any of the originating civilizations of the Western narrative. Second, the varieties of this technology are more multiple and widely distributed, with far more member cultures, than the Eurocentric narrative. And, third, as I shall demonstrate, the bow-under-tension cannot be contained within a single technological trajectory (the arrow as a projectile tool). So, here I shift to a simplified phenomenological analysis of the variations and multistabilies of a first (?) bow-under-tension trajectory.

Four Bow-under-Tension Variations upon Archery

While there are indefinitely many variants upon the bow-under-tension in its archery trajectory, I have chosen here to look at only four that will be at least faintly familiar to the liberally educated reader.

The English Longbow

Technologically, the English longbow is the simplest of the variants here. It was a bow, around six to seven feet long, with bowstring and fletched arrows roughly three feet in length. Its origins stretch back at least 4700 BP and it dominated archery until the late Middle Ages. The most famous longbow military victory was the Battle of Agincourt, in 1415, in which the English army was outmanned three to one, with 5,500 archers facing the crossbow-men of the French. In the end, it is claimed, ten thousand French were slain, and only one hundred English. The longbow was fast to fire—a skilled archer could get five arrows into the air before the first struck—easily taught to foot soldiers, and, producing a hail of arrows, a deadly weapon. Technically, it is a simple device to manufacture; the preferred woods used were yew and ash. Carefully crafted, it was shaped into a shallow "D" form. Its draw averaged seventy pounds and its range 250 meters, with rapid fire capacity.

Figure 14.1. English Longbow.

I now turn to the embodiment practices through which the skills are learned in each variant: The bowman holds the bow in the left hand (if righthanded) with the bow extended in front of his body; the arrow, nocked to the bowstring, is pulled back, with all four fingers doing the pull; the release occurs in conjunction with the desired aim. The process may be repeated rapidly. Clearly, this is a skill that is acquired with long practice; the success rate will be relative to the particular skills of the archer with some better, some worse, than others (Henry VIII was reputedly an excellent archer). To summarize: this bow variant, simple but highly effective, in its human-cultural use entails its own style of embodiment praxis which must take account of the particular materiality of this type of bow.

The Mongolian Horsebow

During the same Medieval period in which the longbow dominated in western Europe, the famed Mongol invaders repeatedly penetrated eastern Europe with an archery radically different, technically and technique-wise, and with equally radically different embodiment practices. Indeed, most Asian and many Middle Eastern archery technologies employed *composite bows*, highly recurved, but with greater firepower than their European counterparts. The bow itself was made with hardwood, bone, and animal sinew, glued with an epoxy-strength fish bladder glue.

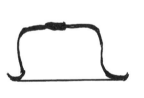 

Figure 14.2. Mongolian Horsebow.

In this variant, I begin with the form of the bow and the cultural reasons for its different shape and composition. In its military use, the Mongolian horsebow was used while the bowman was mounted, and employed in rapid-strike capacities as a cavalry weapon. It should be clear that a longbow would be inconvenient, possibly impossible, to use astride a galloping steed! The recurved, composite bow of the Mongol horseman averaged only three feet in length, but was a much more powerful version of the bow-under-tension. Its range was up to five hundred meters and it had up to a one hundred pound draw.

The embodiment skills needed for mounted attack were drastically different from those used by a standing longbowman. These had to be learned over long periods of time and usually began with young boys. The draw was a simultaneous "push" of the bow away from the body, and a "pull" of the drawstring to cheek position, but often the emphasis was upon the push more than the pull. But the most astonishing skill was to learn how to time the instant of release to happen when all four of the horse's hoofs were off the ground (a moment of no vibration)! The pull was often accomplished with the use of a thumb ring, a device common to many Asian bow practices due to the heavier draw.

This second variation on the bow-under-tension shows a different material technology, a different set of acquired embodiment skills, and a different military use (mounted versus infantry), but the machine itself remains a projectile-delivering device used by archers.

Chinese Artillery Archery

In 2004 I made my first lecture tour to China, with the second stop of the tour a trip to Xi'an, site of the now-famous terra-cotta warriors. This massive 7,500 warrior monument to the Qin Shihuang rule (259–210 BCE [2260 BP]) contains several archers posed in about-to-fire gestures.

Figure 14.3. Xi'an Warrior, Bow Holding.

As in armies everywhere, the hand positions indicate that each war-rior held some kind of weapon, but if these were wooden weapons, they did not survive the twenty-two centuries of burial. The Qin archery, at least thirteen centuries earlier than the Mongol mounted archers, had developed what I call "artillery archery." These bows, compound and recurved like the later Mongol versions, were, like longbows, roughly six feet in length and required the greatest drawing power known in antiquity—more than 160 pounds. (I note in passing that the Qin dynasty also had crossbows of quite sophisticated types, which may have been fired from horse-drawn wagons. An example, in bronze, was found on a chariot within the Xi'an ruins. I am not dealing with crossbows in this context.) These extremely powerful bows called for much muscle power for the embodiment practices needed for skill in this case. No one with less than a weightlifter's muscular capacity could long hold a drawn bow with such pull weight. As with the Mongol horseback versions, these bows called for a push-pull launch, which dif-fered in that the push began with the right arm downward and then during the draw the archer would quickly and simultaneously lift the bow to its artillery position for long range firing (the terra-cotta warriors showed this stance). Also, as with the Mongol version, thumb rings were used to hold the bowstring. The firing range exceeds that of either of the previously noted variants.

Contemporary Compound Complex Bows

The contemporary complex compound bow which adds a cam-pulley system to the drawstring, was a twentieth-century invention, patented by Hol-lis Allen in 1966. Its technology is radically different than classical and ancient bows. Before discussing its material or technical characteristics and the embodiment practices needed, one must also note the general shift in historical context. By the twentieth century the military or weaponry use of the bow-under-tension had for practical purposes, disappeared. Other appli-cations of archery in ancient times, which included hunting, competition, and target practice, remain in place today. The second preliminary note I want to make is that the complex compound bow in its development *employs many of the design features of historical bows and seeks to counteract what are taken as shortcomings.*

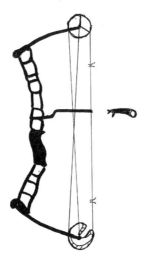

Figure 14.4. Contemporary Compound Bow.

As the illustration shows, the complexity of this bow far exceeds that of classical bows. Gone are the previous materials of wood, bone, sinew, and the like, here replaced by with metal, carbon fiber, or other modern lightweight materials. The bowstring is now strung with double or triple lengths, which go through a set of pulleys or cams that have subvariations (single, hybrid, twin, and binary), each of which produces slightly different effects. But the main difference—which contrasts with all classical bows—is that the draw pull weight remains the same for most of the draw, and it actually lightens slightly at its end extreme. With classical bows, the farther the pull, the greater the power needed, while contemporary bows have adjustable draw weights that rarely exceed seventy pounds. This lighter draw allows more time for aiming adjustment, thereby increasing target accuracy. But in spite of the lighter pull, arrow speed has been substantially increased—compared to classical speeds of 190 feet per second, contemporary speeds can reach up to 260 feet per second. As the illustration shows, other complex additions have been added: the cable rod is designed to allow the arrow to release in such a way that its fletches are not damaged; sighting windows (similar to rifle sights) have been added for aiming; and string silencers have been added to dampen the string "twang" and make for a more silent release.

It is now time to turn to the style of embodiment practices which this bow-under-tension calls for. With this bow, one returns to the longbow stance with a hold in which the bow is held stationary by an outstretched arm; the drawstring is pulled back with the other arm and, with yet another addition, the release is through a mechanical trigger device that holds the drawstring. As noted, time required for aiming is extended due to the stable and lighter pull. And, as with all bow variants, particular embodiment skills must be acquired. These include, of course, individual substyles and ranges of attainments.

These four variants do not exhaust the varieties of bow-under-tension as they have taken shape in different times and cultures. For example, jungle-use bows for which the targets are frequently canopy prey such as birds and monkeys, use much longer arrows than most other archery technologies. Nor have I looked at crossbows, which are also at least a few millennia old and which are complex in different ways than the contemporary bow. However, the four chosen are sufficient to illustrate the invariants and multistabilities of this trajectory of the bow-under-tension.

Invariants of Bow Use

Returning to a phenomenological analysis, I now take note of the invariants that each of the four bow types illustrates. First, in use, the human relationship with the bow-under-tension in its archery trajectory is *interrelational*. If I pick up a bow in any of its variants and I use the bow; the bow also "uses" me. Here the materiality of the bow is bodily-perceptually experienced, but in the different ways that the variants display and allow. Drawing from the limited variants here, both the longbow and the contemporary complex bow have roughly the same draw—which will be experienced by the archer through muscular strain—but in the former case the full exertion builds up, in the second it remains the same throughout the draw. One has to learn the skills for the most efficient, most aesthetic, most accurate firing. There is within this process much *tacit knowledge*, that is, experiential knowledge acquired not through reading a manual or a technical list of capacities, but through the repeated and trained use of the technology. If the bow *reveals* to the user its resistances and accommodations, these are not determinative, although they are distinct. Rather, the archer, or spectrum of archers, can develop nuanced techniques of use—there will be nuanced differences of style, within a range appropriate for the practiced use. And just as with typists or piano players, or bicycle riders, there will be virtuosos and perpetual amateurs. (Or, if we return to the scientific use of *camera obscura* imaging, there will be skilled, perceptive observers and others who can never attain full gestalt attainments. Embodiment effects vary in all human-technology contexts.) The skills attained, following Hubert Dreyfus's skill phenomenology, also become less and less verbal and more and more silently taken for granted within skilled experience. On the material side, a similar progression of refinement can occur with improved and varied instrument shaping—such as arrow points for different purposes, or ever lighter and straighter arrow shafts over time. This is the interactive ontology of human-technology praxis.

The multistability of the set of variants should also be obvious. Each set of archery technologies is embedded within specific cultural contexts; each is adjusted to the complex praxes of organization and use, different for infantry compared to cavalry use, or to the target or hunting uses of the different cultures and times. Yet, abstractly, the *same* bow-under-tension simple machine is at the center of these activities. And in parallel to the visual stabilities of the ambiguous drawings, while there is a very large range of variations (not infinite), each remains different in its assignments. Here, however, the multistabilties are material and embodied, more fully existential than the examples with which experimental phenomenology begins.

Variations of Bow-under-Tension in a Musical Trajectory

Imaginatively, now return to my musical improvisation experience and apply it in an equally imaginative way to *playing* with the bow. I noted how the contemporary complex compound bows have *string silencers*. In all classical bows any archer experiences the "twang" of the bowstring on release. Now, were the practice context to be hunting, this "twang" could be heard by the game, since sound moves faster than the arrow, and one can imagine a deer bolting. But what if one now pays attention to the potentially "musical quality" of the twang? The evidence is ample that our ancestors were highly aware of, and exploited this sound capacity. I will here greatly foreshorten my researches into what I now claim is a quite different *musical trajectory of the bow-under-tension*. Here, rather than work backward as I did in an earlier article, "Technologies—Musics—Embodiments" (*Janus Head* [Oct. 1, 2007]), I shall move historically from the earliest to the contemporary:

Shaman Playing a Bow

The Ice Age was a time of bloom for modern humans in Europe, and while Chauvet Cave is filled with animal depictions from 32,000 BP, a whole series of caves, including *Trois Frères* Cave in southern France, date back to 15,000 BP. In this cave a very large set of animals is depicted, in the midst of which is a human—probably a shaman—who is holding a bow.

Figure 14.5. Trois Frere Cave Shaman with Bow.

I claimed above that the bow-under-tension was at least this old, with some physical evidence of arrows, but here is a depiction of a bow in play. And while ambiguous, most commentators claim that this is a bow in *musical position*; it is clearly *not* in firing position, nor is there an arrow. An intriguing question could be raised: Could what I am calling the musical trajectory of the bow-under-tension have preceded or be as old as the archery trajectory? Probably not, given some evidence that long arrows were propelled by spear throwers earlier, but the question remains intriguing.

Bushman Bow Playing

Much later, and still a practice today, African Bushmen clearly used the "twang" to make music with their unchanged archery bows. On hunts, while marching into the bush, they would play the strings on their bows—and here, again, variations have been noted. J. D. Williams, in "The Art of Music" (*South African Archeological Society Newsletter* [1981], 8 ff.), describes this practice as well as refers to the Bush drawings noted. The string could be *plucked* with a finger, sometimes it was played like a *jaw-harp*, and, with later modifications for more sedentary music making, it could be played with a second, smaller bow.

Bushman rock art found in the Natal Drakensberg   Reproduction by Don Ihde

Figure 14.6. Bushman Cliff Drawings with Bows.

This drawing is of a cliff painting, probably 2,400 BP, in which one can see two adaptive variations upon the hunting bow. The first is the addition of a gourd resonator to amplify the sounds of the string, and the second is the addition of a playing bow to make a more continuous sound. In short, the bow-under-tension is now a single-stringed instrument. Such instruments are still used in both southern Africa and Brazil. This is now clearly within a second instrumental trajectory, a musical trajectory, one that can easily be added to with multiple strings, different resonators, refinements upon bows, and the like.

Before moving farther, I want to note that the musical trajectory—again interrelationally—calls for a different style of embodiment practices. These very simple stringed instruments call for a highly refined playing style precisely because of the limitations in the sounds that can be produced. Ethnomusicologists note that these simple instruments produce subtle overtones, which are, in fact, exploited in the most virtuoso performances of skilled players. One could even claim to some degree that the embodiment skills for such simple instruments must be very highly honed to achieve the best performance. (While not belonging to the string trajectory here, flutes associated with finds from as far back as 45,000 BP have been found whose fingering shows a tuning scale quite similar to more modern scales; here again, the fingering and breath techniques had to be highly refined to produce the best sounds.)

I shall not here undertake more variations or demonstrate that the early, simple modifications to the bow-under-tension could and did lead to the classes of stringed instruments of great cultural-temporal variety in music history. But I will note that there remains the phenomenological pairing of an interrelational development between the material resistances and accommodations of the instruments and the embodied skills of the player in action. And, in parallel to the historical development of imaging technologies, musical technologies undergo adaptations and refinements throughout their histories as well.

Bow-under-Tension in a Tool Trajectory

Return one more time to the improvisation play scenario. While I shall continue my historico-phenomenological narrative, one can imagine that what I am now calling a third technological trajectory gets under way. There is a unique and unusual museum, the Fall River Museum, tucked away within Oxford University's Natural History Museum. The organizers of this museum have organized the multicultural collections of artifacts around certain basic human practices that evolved with virtually every human culture. *Fire making* is one such example. Interestingly, the collection does show a multiple, but finite, number of classical technologies to ignite fires. The most ancient are variations upon "striking" technologies such as flint and metal (steel); others include insulated carrying devices to maintain fire collected from natural sources (volcanoes, lightening strikes, etc.). But variations upon a very widespread and multicultural technology is yet again, *a variation upon the bow-under-tension.* In this case, the modifications to the previous two trajectories begin simply: the string of the firestarter is simply twisted about the arrow analogue. The "arrow" is held down with pressure applied by some sort of mortar or disc-shaped object, and its "point" placed in a piece of wood or other frictionable object, around which is placed carefully laid tinder.

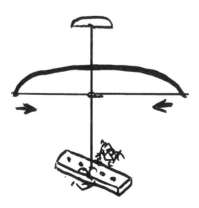

Figure 14.7. Fire Making Bow.

The user then rapidly moves the bow back and forth in an alternating push/pull while pushing down the arrow analogue to produce friction, which soon produces enough heat to light the tinder. (My son Mark learned this skill in wilderness camps and, to the delight of the children in my wife Linda's elementary school, demonstrated that it only took roughly ten seconds to have a fire!) Quickly, and yet again, one can see the simple machine paired with skilled embodiment practices now produces a new *tool trajectory*.

Now, variations: By applying the same push/pull technique with the twisted bow string and using a sharpened arrow point and pressure plate, one has a drill. The ancient Egyptians had such drill devices, another variation in the tool trajectory. Or—and who knows when or where this variation came from?—what if one impregnates the bowstring with an abrasive? Then, this time without the arrow analogue, by push/pull techniques, one has a *sawing tool*. I myself own both antique and modern versions of this bow-under-tension tool.

Figure 14.8. Nineteenth and Twentieth-Century Bowsaws.

Conclusion

The Seventh Machine, bow-under-tension, once again displays the variational set of possibilities claimed by phenomenology, leading to a large set of *multistabilities,* here in an ontological pairing of material configurations in interaction with learned and acquired human embodiment practices. This is also another dimension of an *experimental phenomenology*, now materially embodied as a postphenomenology.

Epilogue

Art, science and philosophy are activities performed by practitioners in communities of discourse. In philosophy the community of discourse is diverse, and not all practitioners understand each others' dialects, nor are the various dances that philosophers perform with mind and mouth the same. It has always been thus, and likely will continue to be so, since philosophies are also variants, though spelled very large. I have tried here to show a few steps in the dance that is phenomenology, but only some elementary ones. I hope there are those who can do the same steps and find in them an excitement and satisfaction that will lead farther. To phenomenology there is no end.

Notes

Chapter One. Introduction

1. For an anthology consisting of the primary authors on the central themes of phenomenology, see Richard M. Zaner and Don Ihde, *Phenomenology and Existentialism* (New York: Capricorn Books, 1973).

2. The three most important works to be cited are: Edmund Husserl, *Ideas: General Introduction to Pure Phenomenology*; Martin Heidegger, *Being and Time*; and Maurice Merleau-Ponty, *Phenomenology of Perception*.

3. Martin Heidegger, *On Time and Being*, translated by Joan Stambaugh (New York: Harper and Row, 1972), 76, 78.

4. Edmund Husserl, *Cartesian Meditations*, translated by Dorion Cairns (The Hague: Martinus Nijhoff, 1960), 153.

5. Martin Heidegger, *Being and Time*, translated by John Macquarrie and Edward Robinson (New York: Harper and Row, 1962), 60.

6. Thomas Kuhn, *The Structure of Scientific Revolutions* (Chicago: University of Chicago Press, 1962).

7. Maurice Merleau-Ponty, *Phenomenology of Perception*, translated by Colin Smith (London: Routledge and Kegan Paul, 1962), 179, 187.

8. For a phenomenological account of auditory experience in contrast, see Don Ihde, *Listening and Voice: A Phenomenology of Sound* (Athens: Ohio University Press, 1976).

Chapter Two. Indians and the Elephant

1. Edmund Husserl, *Cartesian Meditations*, translated by Dorion Cairns (The Hague: Martinus Nijhoff, 1960), 12–13.

2. Martin Heidegger, *Being and Time*, translated by John Macquarrie and Edward Robinson (New York: Harper and Row, 1962), 51.

3. Ibid., 50.

4. Edmund Husserl, *The Crisis of European Sciences and Transcendental Phenomenology*, translated by David Carr (Evanston: Northwestern University Press, 1970), 150.

Chapter Six. Expanded Variations and Phenomenological Reconstruction

1. Many studies have been done on Necker cube reversals. This literature reveals that the implicit assumptions of the researchers have not gone beyond those of their subjects. It tacitly assumes that the odd reversibility of the cube is what is unique about the cube. One study noted that some subjects experienced a flat percept, but explicitly reports it as a hangup associated with fatigue (the Morris article below, 236). See, for representative work, the following three studies in *Perceptual and Motor Skills*: Frank Haronian and A. Arthur Sugarman, "Field Independence and Resistance to Reversal of Perspective," Vol. 22 (1966): 543–46; Helen A. Heath, Dan Erlich, and J. Orbach, "Reversibility of the Necker Cube: Effects of Various Activating Conditions," Vol. 17 (1963): 539–46; and B. B. Morris, "Effects of Order and Trial on Necker Cube Reversals Under Free and Resistive Instructions," Vol. 33 (1971): 235–40.

2. Fred Attneave has discovered limited instances of what he calls "tristable" occurrences, but these are not expanded upon topographically. Fred Attneave, "Multistability in Perception," *Scientific American* 225 (Dec. 1971): 63.

3. Edmund Husserl, *The Crisis*, 150.

Chapter Eight. Projection

1. Fred Attneave, "Multistability in Perception," *Scientific American* (Dec. 1971): 68.

2. See Martin Heidegger, "Conversation with a Japanese," in *On the Way to Language* (New York: Harper and Row, 1971), 1–54.

Chapter Nine. Interdisciplinary Phenomenology

1. Paul Ricoeur's "diagnostics" develop this interdisciplinary approach characteristic of all his work. See especially *Freedom and Nature* (Evanston: Northwestern University Press, 1966), 13–17.

2. Kosta Gavroglu, a research physicist, believes that this is not an accidental trait in seeking microphenomena, but that larger and larger instrumentation will be called for.

3. Patrick Heelan, "Horizon, Objectivity and Reality in the Physical Sciences," *International Philosophical Quarterly* VII (1967): 375–412.

4. Don Ihde, "The Experience of Technology," *Cultural Hermeneutics* 2 (1974): 267–79.

5. Ibid., 271.

6. Ibid., 272.

7. Ibid., 272–73.

8. Ibid., 275–76.

9. Peter L. Berger and Thomas Luckmann, *The Social Construction of Reality* (New York: Doubleday, 1966), 20.

10. Ibid., 21.
11. Ibid., 22.
12. Ibid.
13. Ibid., 23.
14. Ibid., 63.
15. Ibid., 64.
16. Ibid., 65.
17. Ibid., 66.
18. Edward S. Casey, *Imagining: A Phenomenological Study* (Bloomington: Indiana University Press, 1976), 191.
19. Ibid., 178.
20. Ibid., 188.
21. Ibid., 199.
22. Ibid., 200.
23. Ibid., 200–201.
24. Ibid., 179–80.
25. Ibid., 206.
26. Ibid., 207.

Chapter Ten. Pragmatism and Phenomenology

1. Carl Mitcham, quoted in Evan Selinger, *Postphenomenology: A Critical Companion to Ihde* (Bloomington: Indiana University Press, 2006), 22.
2. Richard Rorty, *Concequences of Pragmatism* (Minneapolis: University of Minnesota Press, 1982), 162.
3. Ibid., 162.
4. Ibid., xiv.
5. Ibid., 213–14.
6. Mitcham, op.cit., 31.
7. Ibid., 22.
8. Edmund Husserl. *The Crisis of European Sciences and Transcendental Phenomenology*, trans. David Carr (Evanston: Northwestern University Press, 1970), 353.
9. Ibid.
10. Ibid., 354.
11. Ibid., 370.
12. Mitcham, op.cit., 23.
13. Husserl, *Crisis*, 25.
14. Ibid.
15. Ibid., 26.
16. Ibid., 32.
17. Mitcham, op.cit., 23.
18. Ibid., 26.
19. Ibid.
20. Husserl, *Crisis*, 360–61.

21. Ibid.
22. Ibid.
23. Ibid.

Chapter Thirteen. Variations on the *Camera Obscura*

1. Isaac Newton letters, quoted in "Isaac Newton and Robert Hooke, Dispute on the Nature of Light," in *Galileo's Commandment*, ed. E. B. Bowles (New York: W. H. Freeman, 1997), 184 ff.

2. George Harrison, Richard Lord, and John Loofbourow, *Practical Spectroscopy* (Englewood Cliffs: Prentice-Hall, 1948), 2.

3. Robert Bud and Deborah Warner, eds., *Instruments of Science: A Historical Encylopedia* (New York: Garland, 1998), 563.

4. Jon Darius, *Beyond Vision* (Oxford: Oxford University Press, 1984), 16.

5. www.rleggat.com/photohistory.

6. Ibid.

References

Crowell, Stephan. "The Cartesianism of Phenomenology." *Continental Philosophy Review* 35 (2002): 433–54.

Heidegger, Martin. *Being and Time*. New York: Harper and Row, 1962.

Holenstein, Elmar. *Roman Jakobson's Approach to Language: Phenomenological Structuralism*. Bloomington: Indiana University Press, 1976.

Husserl, Edmund. *The Crisis of European Sciences and Transcendental Phenomenology*. Evanston: Northwestern Univeristy Press, 1970.

Ihde, Don. *Technology and the Lifeworld*. Bloomington: Indiana University Press, 1990.

———. "Husserl's Galileo Needed a Telescope." *Philosophy and Technology* 24, no. 1 (2010).

Mitcham, Carl. *Thinking through Technology*. Chicago: University of Chicago Press, 1994.

———. " From Phenomenology to Pragmatism." In Evan Selinger, *Expanding Postphenomenology: A Critical Companion to Ihde*. Albany: State University of New York Press, 2006.

Rorty, Richard. *The Mirror of Nature*. Chicago: University of Chicago Press, 1979.

———. *Consequences of Pragmatism*. Chicago: University of Chicago Press, 1982.

Teresi, Dick. *Lost Discoveries*. New York: Simon and Schuster, 2002.

Welton, Donn. *The Other Husserl*. Bloomington: Indiana University Press, 2002.

Wilshire, Bruce. *William James and Phenomenology*. Bloomington: Indiana University Press, 1968.

Index